The Blue Badge Guide's
LONDON
Quiz Book

The Blue Badge Guide's
LONDON
Quiz Book

Mark King

This book is dedicated to Londoners who helped my parents make new lives here; my brother Peter who encouraged me into guiding; my family for their generous support; my teachers for their wisdom and inspiration. 'Thank you' to Marc, Philippa, Kieran and Diane for proof-reading and to Nicola for editing.

First published 2016

Reprinted 2016, 2017

The History Press
The Mill, Brimscombe Port
Stroud, Gloucestershire, GL5 2QG
www.thehistorypress.co.uk

© Mark King, 2016

The right of Mark King to be identified as the Author
of this work has been asserted in accordance with the
Copyright, Designs and Patents Act 1988.

All rights reserved. No part of this book may be reprinted
or reproduced or utilised in any form or by any electronic,
mechanical or other means, now known or hereafter invented,
including photocopying and recording, or in any information
storage or retrieval system, without the permission in writing
from the Publishers.

British Library Cataloguing in Publication Data.

A catalogue record for this book is available from the British Library.

ISBN 978 0 7509 6823 2

Typesetting and origination by The History Press
Printed and bound by CPI Group (UK) Ltd

Contents

Foreword

I love quizzes and can be quite argumentative – I was convinced that the second largest private garden is at Lambeth Palace and not the answer given in Tour 1, for example – but now must accept that I never stop learning about London!

This being a quiz book, I'll pose a question of my own.

Why has a non-native Londoner been invited to introduce this collection of tours?

Well, perhaps no one is more qualified than someone who has chosen to spend thirty years working here, who finds London weaving into her identity, and who is passionate in her belief that this is the world's very best city to visit, do business, to study and to enjoy life.

I was born in Sri Lanka and educated in Scotland – my parents' homeland – where I studied German and English Literature, and I've lived in Germany and Australia. The great research I had access to at VisitBritain, the national tourism agency, taught me *'To see oursels as ithers see us'* (to quote Robert Burns), so I claim a broad insight into how London sees itself and is seen by others – for better and for worse.

London is today one of the world's most successful and alluring cities that attracts talent from all over the planet, so it's hard to believe that in the 1980s its population was in decline. Now it's the largest in its history. London has become my home too. I find it endlessly fascinating, and more visitors than ever are also discovering that London is GREAT.

Based on my personal experience and opportunities encountered while working in tourism, I have to say that London's quality of life has improved hugely during my time here – better museums and galleries (many free!); more arts and cultural activity; better care and interpretation of heritage (often thanks to Heritage Lottery Fund investment); cleaner streets and buildings; improved public transport options (and introduction of the handy Oyster card and contactless payment); more spaces for pedestrians; outdoor cafés; a wider range of shops, markets and places to eat; more waymarked walks and cycle ways; welcoming smiles on more peoples' faces; and new neighbourhoods to explore. This is true whether you're a London resident, a visitor from elsewhere in these British Isles or from farther away, here for the first time or back again for more.

This book celebrates so much of London's endlessly rich, ever-changing mix. The cleverly constructed tours certainly inspire me to get out there and explore more of the wider area. I hope they also inspire you to appreciate much more of this wonderful city in the entertaining company of one of London's well-qualified Blue Badge guides!

Sandie Dawe CBE
London & Partners Board Member
www.visitlondon.com
July 2016

Introduction

Have you seen that grapes for sparkling wines are now being grown commercially in Enfield, north London?

Did you know that one of the world's most successful academies for performing artistes is in Croydon, south London?

Or that the largest existing tidal mill in the world is waiting for you in Bow, east London?

Have you visited the UNESCO World Heritage Site in Kew, west London?

In whichever direction you travel, there are fascinating places to see and stories to be discovered – and all this is in addition to many famous sights in central London that help make this the most visited city on our planet. Think of London and it is surely impossible not to conjure up images of Tower Bridge, Buckingham Palace, Big Ben, the River Thames or the British Museum. And yet there is much more waiting to be found a little farther afield.

London's Blue Badge guides are professionally qualified experts, who love helping visitors to discover wonderful places and celebrate their part in London's story. So, instead of a standard quiz made up of lots of Very Interesting Facts about London's well-known tourist sights, this book has been conceived as a series of themed tours that guide you through much more of London's immense variety and sheer extraordinariness.

Imagine yourself exploring London with your very own Blue Badge guide. Your knowledgeable companion will lead you on a series of entertaining tours covering a wide variety of interesting topics. Each of these twenty-two journeys conveniently sidesteps the usual constraints – time and space, past and present – enabling you to explore places you may think you know, or parts of town that are new to you, in complete comfort. These tours travel in all directions and out as far as the M25, the orbital motorway encircling the wider metropolitan area.

Each tour is made up of ten increasingly challenging questions. The answer to Question 1 should be familiar to most visitors and residents, but don't be complacent! If you are still getting correct answers at the end of each tour, you are already well on the way to becoming a London Expert – and we look forward to your application for a place on the next course to qualify as a London Blue Badge guide!

This is no ordinary quiz book because London is no ordinary city. Have fun and do come out and explore!

Mark King
July 2016

Finding a London Blue Badge guide

British Guild of Tourist Guides www.britainsbestguides.org
Guide London/APTG www.guidelondon.org.uk

About the Author

Mark King qualified as a London Blue Badge tourist guide after a thirty-year career in marketing.

Born and raised in suburban north London, he graduated from the University of Oxford with a degree in Modern Languages & Modern History. Mark spent twenty years at one of the world's best-known advertising agencies, then he moved in-house to advise leading international corporate and commercial law firms based in the City of London.

Mark's education and career took him around Britain and overseas, with lengthy assignments in America, Russia and the Czech Republic. He took full advantage of opportunities to explore heritage and contemporary culture in environments as diverse as a New York ad. agency, creative start-ups in post-Communist Prague, St Petersburg and Moscow, a *lycée* in Bordeaux and a *kibbutz* in Israel. Holidays have been spent discovering more of his own country, as well as the wider world, often with the help of professional local guides in fascinatingly varied countries. His travels to date include Egypt, South Africa, Canada, USA, Singapore and Thailand, as well as the four corners of Europe from Poland, Italy, Greece, Malta, to France, Denmark and Germany.

Now a full-time professional guide himself, Mark leads a wide variety of tours within central London and out of town with overseas visitors, British residents of all ages and staff of London businesses. He enjoys experiences of the megacity he calls 'the Big Onion', peeling away layers of history at iconic sights such as Westminster Abbey, as well as in the City of London, Southwark's Bankside, Kenwood House and the King's Cross redevelopment zone. Favourite thematic tours include modern architecture, 'tracking Crossrail', 'Jewish London', and First World War Zeppelin air raids.

He sits on the Executive Council of the British Guild of Tourist Guides, is a member of the Institute of Tourist Guiding, Guide London (Association of Professional Tourist Guides), the City of London Guide Lecturers Association, the Finchley Society and London Historians.

Mark writes quizzes for a community group that raises funds for good causes. He has been an individual winner of Guide London's annual quiz for professional guides and at the time of writing is a member of the winning team.

During two years of intensive study towards qualification for the London Blue Badge – and also the City of London's own guiding qualification, in which he topped his class – his long-suffering family found it necessary to bring in a House Rule that restrained his endless enthusiasm for sharing newly discovered information to no more than 'Three facts a meal'.

Mark is delighted to share his knowledge and passion for London with you now. With considerably more than 220 facts, this book aims to inspire you to discover more of our amazing City in the company of a Blue Badge guide!

www.britainsbestguides.org/guides/3409/mark+king/
www.secret-london.co.uk/Walks_Mark_king_2.html
www.WorldWarOneWalks.com
@MarKomms

TOUR 1

Parks & Gardens

Visitors – and residents – are often delighted to find London is such a green city.

Domestic gardens, public parks, common land, playing fields, nature reserves, 'green roofs', allotments and graveyards mean that approximately half of London is classified as 'green' spaces. By way of comparison, that is equivalent to the entire area of Cape Town or Brussels. Another 2.5% is 'blue' – rivers, canals, ponds and reservoirs.

Before you explore London's greenery with a Blue Badge tourist guide, this round of questions tests just how 'green' you are when it comes to knowing about some of the local parks and gardens.

1   Once a royal hunting estate, London's largest park was opened to the public thanks to an Act of Parliament in 1872. Which is it?

   a. Hyde Park
   b. St James's Park
   c. Hampstead Heath

   d. Richmond Park
   e. Wandsworth Common
   f. Queen's Park

2. Which gardens have been designated as a UNESCO World Heritage Site because of their unique global role in conserving natural biodiversity and promotion of economic botany?

3. Which east London park became Europe's largest new urban park in 150 years after first opening in 2012?

4. Which of the following organisations manages more of Greater London's public open spaces than the others in this list?

   a. The Royal Parks
   b. The National Trust
   c. The City of London Corporation

5. London's principal royal residence at Buckingham Palace and its famous 40-acre gardens are opened to the public each summer. Which private house claims the next largest garden in London?

6. In which London park will you find a Memorial to Heroic Self-Sacrifice?

7. In which park will you see pelicans, whose ancestors were a gift from the Russian Ambassador in 1664?

8. Which park is home to a sculpture of the children's character Peter Pan?

9. Why is there unexpected greenery inside St Dunstan in the East and Christ Church Greyfriars?

10. Which park in west London puts on open-air opera performances?

After that tour of green spaces, the next route introduces some of the communities that make up London.

Answers: Tour 1

1. d. Richmond Park

This park is the largest inside the M25, London's ring road, which will be our outer limit on these tours. Covering an area equivalent to 1,150 football pitches, Richmond Park is three times the size of New York's Central Park. Attractions include ancient trees, wildlife habitats, sports facilities, open-water swimming, superb views of central London, and herds of deer, whose ancestors were hunted by King Henry VIII in the sixteenth century.

2. The Royal Botanic Gardens, Kew

Created in 1759, Kew Gardens has developed into a vital centre for the study, conservation, economic management and simple enjoyment of plants from all around the world. In addition to a research centre, the 300-acre gardens display more than 30,000 plant types enjoyed by 2 million visitors each year.

3. The Queen Elizabeth Olympic Park

Venue for an unforgettable festival of sport during the Olympic and Paralympic Games of London 2012, the 560-acre site – the size of Monaco – was then remodelled and renamed in honour of our sovereign in the 60th year of her reign. It even acquired a new postcode – E20 – coincidentally the same as fictional Walford from BBC TV's long-running series *EastEnders*.

4. c. The City of London Corporation

The Open Spaces department of The City of London Corporation – the administrative body for London's financial district – manages 11,250 acres of historic and natural open space for public recreation and health. That's the equivalent of half of a town the size of Florence, Italy. Green spaces such as Hampstead Heath (just 4 miles from Trafalgar Square), Epping Forest (concealing legendary highwayman Dick Turpin's hideout) and city-centre pocket gardens are maintained chiefly from the Corporation's resources and supported by donations, sponsorship, grants and trading income.

5. Winfield House

Residence of the Ambassador of the United States of America, Winfield House is an elegant villa set in 12 acres of private grounds. That is equivalent to eight football pitches, or in this case let's say nine American football fields. It was gifted in 1946 by Barbara Hutton, heiress of Frank Winfield Woolworth, the American retail tycoon. The house and gardens are located in Regent's Park, the remainder of which is open to the public. Almost as large as the ambassador's garden is the archbishop's at Lambeth Palace – more than 10 acres in size and also wholly worth a visit.

6. Postman's Park off St Martin's-le-Grand, EC1

Brainchild of celebrated nineteenth-century painter G.F. Watts, this quirky memorial celebrates the heroism of ordinary people, who gave their lives attempting to save others. The scheme has been restarted recently and the first modern ceramic panel records a brave individual who died in 2007.

7. St James's Park

London's first colony of pelicans was an unconventional gift from Russia to King Charles II. Highly visible among the extensive bird-life on the lake near Buckingham Palace, numbers swelled in 2013 with the gift of white pelicans by the Czech city of Prague.

8. Kensington Gardens

Legend has it that author of the Peter Pan stories, J.M. Barrie, secretly arranged for a statue of his famous 'boy who never grew up' to fly in to the park overnight to surprise children – and adults – in the morning. He lived across the road from the park gates, by the way. This park boasts many varieties of water fowl and birds, as well as mature trees and colourful ornamental flower beds.

9. Conserved as memorial gardens

Both churches suffered extensive damage from enemy bombing during the Second World War. Rather than rebuild for worship, their deconsecrated naves have been transformed into public gardens and memorials.

10. Holland Park

Holland House was a grand town house famous in political and cultural circles since as early as the eighteenth century. Managed by the Royal Borough of Kensington & Chelsea, its grounds are now a beautiful public open space. The park's popular season of opera performances is a perfect accompaniment to London's warm summer evenings (but bring a blanket, just in case).

TOUR 2

People & Populations

People from within these islands and from overseas have been coming and going for 2,000 years. London's population has never been larger – 8.6m and growing, plus several million in the wider metropolitan area – and is the most diverse community in Britain; nearly four in ten residents were born abroad. Today, more than 300 languages are spoken by children attending London's schools.

Here's an introduction to a few of the communities living in this capital city:

1. Which empire established Londinium as capital of the province of Britannia after invading in AD 43?

2. Which conquering army built the White Tower in the castle known today as the Tower of London?

3. James I became King of England on the death of Queen Elizabeth I. In which country is he known as James VI?

4. In which of these boroughs is 'Banglatown', the heart of London's modern Bengali community?

   a. Ealing
   b. Barnet
   c. Kensington & Chelsea
   d. Westminster
   e. Tower Hamlets
   f. Merton

5. Settlers from which country are the link between the following objects and people?

   - The districts of Clapham and Cricklewood
   - Navigation canals
   - Eliza Doolittle in *Pygmalion* (also *My Fair Lady*)
   - Guinness Extra Stout

6. What immigrant group is commemorated by the Kindertransport memorial at Liverpool Street station?

7. True or false? The statue of US President George Washington in Trafalgar Square stands on American soil.

8. Settlers from which country helped establish the following customs, expertise and fashions?

   - Blue & white pottery
   - Santa Claus
   - Auctions
   - Gin
   - Tulips
   - 'Total Football'

9. King Charles II's wife, Catherine of Braganza, was a princess from which country?

10. Suite 212 in Claridge's Hotel was briefly part of which continental European nation?

*Now that you've been introduced to some local folk,
let's get ready for the next tour.*

Answers: Tour 2

1. Roman

Thank the Romans that we have a city at all, because there is no evidence of a permanent settlement on this site before their conquest. Following conquest anybody who wanted to be a somebody longed to say *Civis Romanus sum* ('I am a Roman citizen') and we still find their Latin legacy today.

2. The Normans from north France

1066 is a Very Important Date in England's history. Conquest by Duke William's army led to far-reaching changes in monarchy, government, land-holding, culture, architecture and language. The White Tower was built soon after to keep an eye on London's feisty merchants, while simultaneously defending its riches from attack up the River Thames.

3. Scotland

A separate kingdom until the Act of Union in 1707, Scotland's king succeeded England's 'Virgin Queen' on her death in 1603 – a fateful irony, as in 1587 Elizabeth had authorised execution of his mother, Mary, Queen of Scots. In 1612, James reburied his mother's body in the royal church of Westminster Abbey on the opposite side of the very chapel where Elizabeth is buried.

4. Tower Hamlets

The area around Brick Lane in Tower Hamlets is the centre of London's Bengali and Sylheti communities.

While people from different nations and cultures live alongside each other all across London, Ealing is home to many people from Polish and Indian backgrounds; Barnet has numerous Jewish and Japanese residents; large numbers of Russian and Arabic-speaking people are concentrated in Kensington & Chelsea; Europe's largest Chinese community is in Westminster; and Merton has many Korean residents.

5. Ireland

People of Irish descent constitute one of the largest communities in London. Cricklewood is a north-western district with a well-established Irish presence, with Clapham lately developing an Irish identity. Many Irish arrived in England in the eighteenth and nineteenth centuries to work as 'navvies' digging the network of inland canals (navigation channels) that transformed industrial transportation. Eliza Doolittle is the heroine of Irish-born playwright George Bernard Shaw's play *Pygmalion*, later made into a successful musical and film *My Fair Lady*. And if you didn't know that Guinness is Irish beer, it's time you visited one of London's fine pubs. *Sláinte*!

6. Jewish children rescued between 1938–39

The Kindertransport were specially chartered trains that rescued 10,000 Jewish children from Nazi Germany, Austria, Czechoslovakia and the Free City of Danzig shortly before the Second World War. Trains from sixteen cities involved in this rescue mission arrived here, where refugee children were placed in foster homes, on farms or in hostels. The memorial is by sculptor Frank Meisler, who escaped from

Danzig (Gdansk in modern Poland) on one of the final trains; the young girl in his composition is modelled on a member of his own family.

This twentieth-century chapter of immigration continued a story of Jewish presence in England since the Normans in the eleventh century, although the community had been expelled between 1290 and the mid-1650s. A major wave of Jewish immigration from Russia and Eastern Europe also occurred between the 1880s and 1905.

7. False (probably!)

A legend claims that at the time of the revolutionary wars to create an independent nation out of Britain's American colonies, Washington expressed delight that he would '*Never set foot in London again*'. And so, when the state of Virginia later gifted a bronze statue to London, it was accompanied by a consignment of native soil to ensure the first US President stood forever on anything but enemy dirt.

That certainly makes a great story, but there is no gritty evidence and plenty of Americans have chosen to make London their home these days.

8. The Netherlands/Holland

Dutch-born King William of Orange and his English-born wife, Queen Mary II, came to the throne following the 'Glorious Revolution' of 1688. With their court came a mania for all things Dutch including Delft pottery, tulip-growing and, more ruinously, gin ('*genever*'). In Dutch auctions, prices decrease incrementally instead of rising, until a buyer is found. Santa Claus ('Sinterklaas' or 'Sint Nicholaas') became popular here in the nineteenth century.

'Total Football' was a late twentieth style, sadly never adopted successfully by English teams!

9. Portugal

The Anglo–Portuguese alliance of 1386 is said to be the oldest still in force anywhere in the world. These days, Portuguese residents are numerous in Vauxhall, Lambeth and Brent, with many Portuguese-speaking Brazilians in Bayswater and Stockwell.

10. Yugoslavia

Alexander, Crown Prince of Yugoslavia – also named Alexander II Karađorđević – was born during his parents' exile in London during the Second World War. Officially ceding the space temporarily was an elegant solution to the requirement that a Yugoslav sovereign must be born on Yugoslav soil.

Crime & Punishment

This round of questions may prove to be a bit of a trial, as it cross-examines your knowledge of 'legal London'. 'Capital punishment', one might say.

1. By which name is the Central Criminal Court – London's principal criminal court building – popularly known?

   a. Old Nick
   b. Old Holborn
   c. Old Lang Syne
   d. Old Bailey
   e. Old Street

2. What is the name of the legal district south of the Royal Courts of Justice?

3. In which century were the most people executed inside the notorious Tower of London?

   a. sixteenth
   b. seventeenth
   c. eighteenth
   d. nineteenth
   e. twentieth

4. Which politician's name is used familiarly to mean a police officer?

5. In long-running science fiction TV series *Dr Who*, the main character travels through time and space in a blue box he calls the 'Tardis'. What was its original function?

6. Match the form of punishment with the London location.

   a. Hanging, drawing and quartering
   b. Hanging on the gallows
   c. Execution by gladiatorial combat
   d. Exile to the colonies
   e. Imprisonment for debt
   f. Public beheading
   g. Hanging for piracy

   i. Tower Hill
   ii. Millbank
   iii. Tyburn
   iv. Smithfield
   v. Marshalsea
   vi. Amphitheatre
   vii. Execution Dock

7. What is the name of the Bishop of Winchester's former lock-up in Bankside?

8. Why would you not want to meet the Scavenger's Daughter?

9. Which court is based in the former Middlesex Guildhall building in Parliament Square?

10. Which large London prison has a public restaurant run by prisoners?

Hopefully that was not too painful after all!
We've served our time and now need to move on.

Answers: Tour 3

1. d. Old Bailey

The most famous criminal court in the world with a much-photographed statue symbolising Justice on its roof, London's Central Criminal Court is located on a street called Old Bailey. Opened in 1907 on the site of the notorious Newgate Gaol and execution site, no guided tour of 'legal London' would be complete without seeing this courthouse or even sitting in on one of the trials.

2. The Temple

The High Court and Court of Appeal moved in 1882 from Westminster to G.E. Street's cathedral-like Royal Courts of Justice on Strand. Lawyers had been based in the area since the fourteenth century, when land was granted after suppression of the Knights Templar, an order of chivalry whose legacy lives on in the area's name.

3. e. The twentieth century

In spite of its gruesome reputation as a place of imprisonment, punishment and execution, relatively few people are believed to have been put to death within the Tower's precincts. This 'privilege' appears to have been restricted to high-profile or sensitive cases involving members of the Royal Family or nobility, until during the First and Second World Wars when a dozen prisoners found guilty of espionage were executed by firing squad.

4. Sir Robert 'Bobby' Peel (1788–1850)

Peel was Home Secretary when the Metropolitan Police Force was established in 1829. Once known as 'Peelers', 'Bobbies' soon became the nickname for police officers. With their reputation for helpfulness, London's blue-uniformed bobbies have become as much a part of London's iconography as red buses.

5. On-street police telephone call box

A common sight when the BBC's TV series debuted in the 1960s, The Doctor's fictional mode of transport has become hard to find in reality. The name means 'Time And Relative Dimension In Space', so ask your guide to make time to travel to a space just outside Earl's Court Tube station, where you will find one of these rare curiosities.

6. a. – iv; b. – iii; c. – vi; d. – ii; e. – v; f. – i; g. – vii

Hanging, drawing and quartering in medieval London in the area close to the butchery of Smithfield livestock and meat market seems inhumanely apposite.

Common criminals were hung on the large, triangular gallows known as 'Tyburn Tree' from the twelfth-eighteenth centuries. Then a public spectacle, today the site is discreetly marked on a traffic island near busy Marble Arch roundabout.

Roman prisoners suffered ordeal by gladiatorial combat in Londinium's amphitheatre.

Millbank Penitentiary in Chelsea was a holding pen and departure point for nineteenth-century convicts sentenced to exile in penal colonies on the other side of the world.

The Marshalsea was a debtors' prison in Southwark. The father of 12-year-old Charles Dickens was held here pending repayment of debts, a bitter experience echoed in the Victorian author's later novel *Little Dorrit*, set in the local area.

Beheadings of prisoners held in the Tower of London took place in the large, public space close by on Tower Hill. Today, the venue is marked by a dignified plaque commemorating more than 125 executions.

Piracy, smuggling and mutiny at sea were capital crimes punishable by hanging, and Wapping's Execution Dock was kept busy between the fifteenth and nineteenth centuries. A short rope was used to prolong the agony of asphyxiation, then the body left to moulder in an iron cage for three tides to wash over it, as notorious pirate Captain Kidd discovered.

7. The Clink
Yes, this is believed to be the origin of the phrase 'in the clink' (locked up in jail). A twelfth-century bishop built a small lock-up in the grounds of his London residence, where local ne'er-do-wells were held, until the prison was destroyed in a notorious riot in 1780. The name comes from either the metallic clang of a blacksmith's hammer when clapping prisoners in irons, or a Flemish word for the door-latch that deprived them of their freedom. You are at liberty today to ask your guide to show you around.

8. It is a torture device
Also known as the 'Spanish Cravat' or 'Skeffington's Irons' (after a sixteenth-century gaoler), this metal device pulled the victim's head into an increasingly uncomfortable position by their legs, in order to inflict suffering or extract confession. On a guided tour in the Tower of London it will not hurt you to visit a room displaying historic instruments of torture.

9. The Supreme Court

The UK's highest court hears appeals on arguable points of law of the greatest public importance for the whole of the United Kingdom in civil cases, and for England, Wales and Northern Ireland in criminal cases. It is open to visit.

10. HMP Brixton

Run by the Clink charity as a rehabilitation scheme for offenders serving a prison sentence and aimed at preventing reoffending by equipping them with useful skills, HMP Brixton's Clink restaurant is open to the public for bookings by prior arrangement. This successful initiative is modelled on a small number of prison restaurants set up around the country and Brixton is the first one in London.

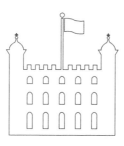

TOUR 4

Writers & Artists

Writers and artists have been recording life here through the years and play a major part in documenting the city today. It's time to take a tour looking at men and women in the Arts.

1. Which diarist recorded life in London during the Great Plague of 1665 and Great Fire of 1666?

2. In which square stands the Fourth Plinth, home to a dynamic series of commissioned artworks?

3. Which prolific novelist and chronicler of Victorian London lived at 48 Doughty Street WC1?

4. Which world-famous detective writer developed a helpful knowledge of poisons while working at a leading London hospital?

5. Which children's hospital benefits from a generous assignment of royalty rights for *Peter Pan* by playwright Sir J.M. Barrie?

6. Which eighteenth-century artist painted *A Rake's Progress* displayed in Sir John Soane's Museum in Lincoln's Inn Fields?

7. Which artist painted the interior dome of St Paul's Cathedral and the Painted Hall of the Greenwich Hospital?

8. Name the UK's largest sculpture, created by Sir Anish Kapoor and Cecil Balmond in 2012.

9. Name the London-born artist, whose signature work *My Bed* is in Tate Britain's collection.

10. Which Anglo-Bangladeshi writer chronicled twentieth-century life on Brick Lane, the heart of London's Banglatown?

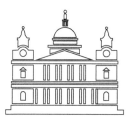

Did you get all the 'write' answers?
Our next tour explores what some of
London's words and names are all about.

Answers: Tour 4

1. Samuel Pepys (1633-1703)

Moving in high social circles, Pepys ('Peeps') became a senior official in the Admiralty. He was an acute observer who recorded his impressions in a coded diary kept from 1660-1669. His decoded writings have given us a fascinating account of Restoration-era daily life, turbulent politics and historic events, although the jottings about his marital infidelities clearly were never intended for anyone else's eyes.

2. Trafalgar Square

The redeveloped square's north-western plinth was never occupied by its intended royal statue and remained empty until the late 1990s, since when a succession of artworks have been displayed. This successful and thought-provoking scheme managed by the Mayor of London's Culture Team commissions world-class artworks for the public realm from leading artists. 2015's display was the subversive *Gift Horse* by Hans Haacke, with *Really Good*, a giant thumbs-up from David Shrigley, put up in 2016.

3. Charles Dickens

No tour of 'literary London' could be complete without taking in some of the many sites associated with Charles Dickens. 48 Doughty Street was his family home from 1837-39 and now houses an excellent museum celebrating his life, works and influence.

4. Dame Agatha Christie (1890-1976)

Using various pen-names as author of more than ninety titles including the 'Hercule Poirot' and 'Miss Marple' series, Christie has sold more than 2 billion books worldwide. She also holds the record for the world's longest unbroken run of a play: *The Mousetrap* opened in the West End in 1952. Her memorial is on the corner of Cranbourn Street and Great Newport Street in the heart of Theatreland. Ask your guide to track down locations used in the many TV and film adaptations of her work.

5. Great Ormond Street Hospital for Children

After becoming a committed supporter of its work, Barrie assigned a revenue stream from his famous play to this leading London children's hospital in 1929, having no children of his own. The hospital continues to benefit today. Other famous literary benefactors include Charles Dickens, who even mentions it in his novel *Our Mutual Friend*. 'GOSH!'

6. William Hogarth (1697-1764)

London-born Hogarth's series of eight paintings tells the story of Tom Rakewell, who inherits a fortune from his miserly father only to embark upon a tragic spiral towards vice and self-destruction. Be warned!

A leading architect in his day, Sir John Soane (1753-1837) acquired Hogarth's 'modern, moral subject' for his country house in Ealing, before moving it to his central London residence.

7. Sir James Thornhill (1675?-1734)

Thornhill developed a reputation painting large-scale compositions in the baroque style and his best-known works grace two of London's grandest buildings: the City of London's cathedral and the former seamen's retirement home in Greenwich. Both sites welcome visitors. Incidentally, Thornhill depicted himself – hand outstretched – in his great mural at Greenwich and was father-in-law to William Hogarth.

8. ArcelorMittal Orbit

Inside this 376ft twisted metal red sculpture is an observation platform with views over and beyond the Queen Elizabeth Olympic Park. The structure was designed as a publicly accessible artwork and centrepiece during – and after – London's Olympic and Paralympic Games. Stretched out vertically the twisted, red steel structure would be taller than Paris's Eiffel Tower, so the announcement that it has been fitted with the world's longest helter-skelter slide has will be welcomed by big kids of all ages.

9. Tracy Emin (1963-)

Croydon-born 'Young British Artist' Tracy shot to fame around the time when her deceptively messy-looking installation *My Bed* was shortlisted for the prestigious Turner Prize. In 2007, Tracy represented Britain in the Venice Biennale. With a studio in Spitalfields, Emin is established as a leading player in London's vibrant modern art scene and continues to challenge conventions in her works of painting, drawing, video, installation, photography, needlework and sculpture.

10. Monica Ali (1967-)

Born in Dhaka, Bangladesh, Monica's breakthrough novel *Brick Lane* was shortlisted for the coveted Man Booker Prize and later adapted into a film. The novel is set in east London's Sylheti community around Brick Lane and explores the process of a young female immigrant adapting to life in Britain.

Find portraits in paint and photo of many great London writers and artists in the National Portrait Gallery, and explore London's vibrant art scene in galleries and museums or out on the streets with an expert Blue Badge guide.

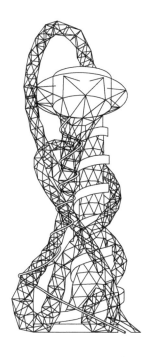

TOUR 5

Words & Meanings

As if it were not enough to find over 300 languages spoken nowadays in London – fifty-three of which are classified by the Office for National Statistics as 'main languages' – the fabric of our global city is scattered with traces of languages and words that evolved into their modern usage.

This set of questions peels away 2,000 years of etymological history and introduces you to the unique sound of Londoners' own dialect, Cockney.

1. The name of which famous Westminster street derives from the Old English word for 'river bank'?

2. Cheapside was one of medieval London's main market streets. It is self-explanatory what was sold on Honey Lane, Bread Street, Ironmonger Lane or Wood Street, but who traded on Friday Street?

3. In Londoners' traditional dialect of Cockney-rhyming slang, what is your 'Barnet'?

4. After what or whom is Cannon Street named?

   a. Gun-makers   d. Candle-makers
   b. Priests or canons   e. Sir Septimus Carr-Nunn
   c. Candy-makers

5. Name a street near St James's Palace that originates with a ball and mallet game played in the seventeenth century by royalty and nobility.

6. True or false? Hackney carriages (taxis) are named after the north London suburb of Hackney.

7. The trading heart of Anglo-Saxon Lundenwic was outside the former Roman city in the area called Aldwych. What does 'Aldwych' mean?

8. A royal road through Hyde Park was once known as *'Route du roi'*. What has its name evolved into today?

9. Smithfield was the site of knights' jousting tournaments. What golden prize is recalled in the name of one of the area's modern streets?

10. Which south London district shares its name with one of the best-selling brands of British car?

Now that we all understand each other so much better, let's find out about our next tour ...

Answers: Tour 5

1. Strand

Following the line of a Roman road along the bank above the river, since Saxon times Strand has been a principal link between the merchant community in the City of London and the royal district of Westminster.

2. Fishmongers

Located near to the river, fishmongers traded on Friday Street – named after the week-day when devout Christians abstained from eating meat. 'Chepe' means 'market' and many ancient English market towns may be identified even today by the word 'Chipping' in their name, for example Chipping Barnet.

3. Hair

A horse and cattle market with a popular fun fair has taken place since 1588 under Royal Charter in the northern suburban town of Chipping Barnet. Londoners speaking in Cockney slang take a word or phrase then rhyme it, often also dropping the very word that rhymes, in this case shortening 'Barnet Fair'. So, 'Nice Barnet, shame about the Boat Race' means that the speaker thinks that person has nice hair but not such a good-looking face ('Oxford and Cambridge University boat race')!

We'll be taking a 'butcher's' ('hook', a look) at outer suburbs like Barnet on our other tours too.

4. d. Candle-makers

Located in the EC4 district, Cannon Street was originally named 'Candlewick Street'. The meeting hall of The Tallow (animal fat) Chandlers Company has been in the area for centuries. The presence of ancient trade organisations known as livery companies or guilds – such as these candle-makers – is found all over the city. They still play an active part in London's commercial and charitable life, as well as its local government and pageantry.

5. Pall Mall and The Mall

Deriving from stick and ball games imported from conti-nental Europe, such as Italian *palla a maglio* and French *paille maille* or *jeu de mail*, a game similar to croquet or golf was once played on long alleys in this royal quarter. These alleys eventually became the streets we know as Pall Mall and The Mall.

6. False

Hacquenée is an old French word meaning an all-purpose horse or 'ambling nag' that pulled London's taxi carriages for three centuries. Of course, this was all before the advent of those 101hp TX4 black cabs that gallop around our streets today in the careful hands of legendarily knowledgeable licensed drivers.

7. Old market settlement

West of today's City of London and on the eastern end of Strand, seafarers and river traders used the Thames to transport their wares. Lundenwic – meaning Lunden trading settlement – took over from Londinium as the name for this city for a period between the departure of the Roman army in 410 and Norman invasion in 1066.

8. Rotten Row

The road taken by King William III to his palace at Kensington in the late seventeenth century is said to have been one of the very first streets to have permanent lighting. Maybe Londoners were just not very bright when it came to pronouncing foreign words!

9. Giltspur Street

Named after 'smooth fields' just outside the city walls, Smithfield was the venue for a tiltyard, where medieval knights displayed their military prowess by spurring on their horse and unseating opponents with their lance. This street was also once known as Knightrider's Street.

10. Vauxhall

London was a major industrial city well into the twentieth century, leaving a rich heritage to discover. Nowadays a division of US automotive giant General Motors working closely with German sister company Opel, Vauxhall began production in south London on land named after thirteenth-century French mercenary soldier Falkes de Breauté, who built a large hall of residence – Falkes Hall. His griffin symbol lives on in Vauxhall's badge, even though manufacturing has moved out of London – in fact, on to land that was also once part of Falkes' estate.

And to understand why the Russian word for a large station is pronounced 'vok-zahl', you'll have to ask your Blue Badge guide!

TOUR 6

Borough & City

London's expansion over nearly 2,000 years has swallowed up once outlying villages and given birth to new neighbourhoods. This tour digs into the foundations of ten districts.

1. Which church gave its name to the City of Westminster?

2. Why is London's financial and business district known as 'the Square Mile'?

3. The district of Blackfriars is named after medieval 'black frères' – Roman Catholic monks who built a substantial monastery near the Thames. To which order of monks did they belong?

   a. Augustinian   d. Cistercian
   b. Dominican   e. Trappist
   c. Carthusian

4. Why are there thirty-two passenger capsules on the London Eye?

5. True or false? Teddington means 'tide turn town'.

6. How did the entertainment district known as Soho get its name?

   a. It is located south of Houston Street
   b. As a market garden, it was frequently sown and hoed
   c. It was the second-hand garment district where tailors sewed up holes in clothing
   d. It is on land once owned by Sir Hugh d'Eaulx
   e. It is named after a shout made by hunters

7. One of these London districts was not developed by members of the Grosvenor family, currently headed by Gerald, 6th Duke of Westminster. Which district?

   a. Chelsea   c. Mayfair
   b. Belgravia   d. Pimlico

8. Which king gave his name to the area known as King's Cross?

9. Which country's embassy is pioneering the development of a new diplomatic quarter in the south London area of Nine Elms?

10. For members of which profession were the fine villas around Melbury Road in Holland Park developed in the late nineteenth century?

Well, we certainly covered a lot of ground on that tour! Time for a short rest before we head off again.

Answers: Tour 6

1. Westminster Abbey

Literally meaning 'the minster [large monastic church] in the west', at a time when London's principal commercial and residential centre was farther east along the river.

2. The City of London is built over the original Roman settlement of Londinium that was surrounded by a city wall, enclosing a surface area of approximately 1 square mile

Since the late twentieth century, a related financial centre has been developing in the former Docklands district known as Canary Wharf, physically outside the 'Square Mile' but included in its wider definition as London's financial sector.

3. b. Dominican

Dominican brothers wore black robes. Monasteries and nunneries were important religious and political centres until the break with the Catholic Church in the early sixteenth century that led to a period of religious persecution and counter-persecution. Discover their legacy today in stories of those troubled times, as well as in names of buildings, districts and streets that are rich in history including Blackfriars, Austin Friars and St Bartholomew the Great. You'll soon get the habit.

4. They represent the thirty-two London boroughs

London is sub-divided into thirty-three administrative districts – the City of London and thirty-two boroughs. Triskaidekaphobic visitors will be relieved to know that on this viewing platform, the capsules are numbered 1-33 but superstition means that there is no capsule 13.

5. False
Situated 55 miles from the river estuary, the west London town of Teddington is said to mark the point where the mighty Thames ceases to be tidal. An impressive early nineteenth-century system of lock-gates does break the river's natural, tidal ebb and flow, but its ancient name is more likely to derive from 'Tudda's ton' – settlement of Tudda's people. Either way, a leisurely cruise along the Thames is a great way to experience life along the banks of London's historic superhighway.

6. e. It is named after a shout made by hunters
The word appears in the early seventeenth century as a hunting cry and was perhaps used by sportsmen chasing rabbits and wildfowl that abounded in the local fields. Today, Soho teems with life both day and night with cafés, bars, restaurants, clubs and many other attractions.

If you chose a. you're thinking of the SoHo district in New York!

7. a. Chelsea.
Arriving with the invading Norman army in the eleventh century, the Grosvenor family later developed land acquired through a judicious marriage in 1677 to London heiress Mary Davies. These areas became today's Mayfair, Belgravia and Pimlico and much of it is still owned by the Grosvenor Estate.

Grosvenor is one of several 'great estate' landowners that have overseen the orderly development of central London, including Cadogan (Chelsea and Knightsbridge), Crown (Regent Street area and Royal Parks), Portman (west Marylebone) and Howard de Walden (east Marylebone). Sometimes described as a city made up of a series of villages, a guided tour of London's great estates interprets this distinctive model of architectural and social diversity.

8. George IV

Before railways, the New Road that forms Marylebone Road, Euston Road and Pentonville Road was considered the northern edge of central London. The land beyond featured in a grandiose, green-field development scheme championed by the Prince Regent – later to reign as King George IV – and his architect, John Nash. For a few years before its removal, a large statue of the king was erected on a road in the area. Today George's legacy lives on more subtly in the name of that area, as well as Regent Street and Regent's Park, an area sometimes referred to as 'Nashville'.

9. United States of America

Embassy Gardens is one of the developments driving regeneration of a large riverside area around the long-disused Battersea Power Station. The American embassy will be leaving Mayfair in 2017, when the Dutch embassy reportedly also will be moving here; other countries are also considering relocation. Battersea-Nine Elms is powering innovative regeneration of this central south-western district, with important commissions for leading international architects, engineers and urban planning consultancies.

10. Artists

Centred today on the former studio-home of celebrated painter Lord Leighton, President of the Royal Academy 1878-96, an artists' colony developed in this upscale west London neighbourhood that attracted leading painters and sculptors, such as G.F. Watts. A walk through Holland Park and streets around Melbury Road will put you in the frame for a tour inside Leighton House.

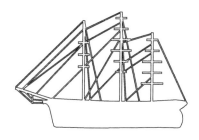

TOUR 7

War & Peace

Our next tour looks at aspects of London that have been influenced by the country's wars or by attempts to bring peace.

1. Which admiral stands on top of a tall stone column in Trafalgar Square?

2. True or false? The Cenotaph in Whitehall commemorating our 'Glorious Dead' is decorated with religious symbols representing leading faiths.

3. Match these British armed forces with their London museum or monument.

   a. Foot Guards
   b. Royal Fusiliers
   c. Household Cavalry
   d. Brigade of Gurkhas
   e. Royal Artillery
   f. Royal Air Force
   g. Royal Navy

   i. Hendon
   ii. Hyde Park Corner
   iii. HMS *Belfast*
   iv. Wellington Barracks, Birdcage Walk
   v. Tower of London
   vi. Horseguards Avenue, Whitehall
   vii. Horse Guards, Whitehall

4. True or false? The first deadly bombing raids on London took place in 1940 during 'the Blitz'.

5. Which victorious general made Apsley House in Piccadilly his home in 1817?

6. Where in London did the first ever General Assembly of the United Nations take place in 1946?

7. Which south London museum records the impact of conflicts in the twentieth and twenty-first centuries?

8. HMS *President* (formerly HMS *Saxifrage*) is moored on the north bank of the Thames in Blackfriars. In which war did it first see active service?

9. What victims of war are commemorated in a striking memorial on Park Lane, W1?

10. To what is the Buddhist temple dedicated that stands on the riverside in Battersea Park, south London?

This seems a suitably positive point to end this tour.

Answers: Tour 7

1. Admiral Lord Horatio Nelson (1758-1805)

Nelson joined the navy aged 12. He rose through the ranks to become Britain's premier naval commander and dashing military hero by the time of his much-lamented death at the Battle of Trafalgar, when his inspiration and daring tactics helped defeat the combined French and Spanish fleets. By the way, the uniform he was wearing when he received that fatal shot is on display at the National Maritime Museum, Greenwich.

2. False

Meaning 'empty tomb' in Greek, Sir Edwin Lutyens' stone memorial replaced a temporary structure in 1920 as the permanent focus for remembering servicemen and women killed in war. This inclusive centrepiece of annual commemorative events for all people in Britain and the Commonwealth carries no religious symbols of any kind.

3. a. – iv; b. – v; c. – vii; d. – vi; e. – ii; f. – i; g. – iii

4. False

The first air raids on London took place in 1915 during the First World War. Zeppelin airships carried out deadly raids with relative impunity until local air defences were strengthened. Fixed-wing bomber aircraft were then introduced, well before the long-running 'Blitz' of the Second World War deployed bombers, V1 jet-propelled flying bombs and V2 supersonic rockets.

5. 1st Duke of Wellington (1769–1852)

The Irish-born soldier Arthur Wellesley saw action in India and continental Europe before rising to command Allied forces that defeated Napoleonic France and its allies in the Iberian Peninsula. In 1815, the recently ennobled Duke led Allied forces at the final defeat of Napoleon Bonaparte in Belgium at the Battle of Waterloo, assisted by the timely arrival of Prussian forces. 'Give me night or give me Blücher', Wellington said at a critical juncture, before giving the boot to 'Boney'. A grateful nation soon gave Wellington lavish funds to build an estate, with which he bought Apsley House. Its understated address: 'Number 1, London.'

This fine mansion tells his story and showcases magnificent gifts bestowed by grateful monarchs. Plenty of bling-bling in these glittering interiors, so bring your sunglasses!

6. Methodist Central Hall, Westminster

Before moving to its permanent home in New York, the General Assembly met in the Methodists' capacious hall opposite Westminster Abbey. A plaque on the Tothill Street side of this building records that optimistic dawn in world affairs.

7. Imperial War Museum

Based in Lambeth, the museum's extensive collection and display spaces document conflicts and wartime experiences in which Britain has been involved during the past century. Its other sites in the London area include HMS *Belfast* on the Thames and Churchill War Rooms in Whitehall.

8. The First World War

Built in 1918 as one of the first of a new type of war-ship – a 'Q-Ship' designed for anti-submarine patrols, a role later taken by frigates. The last remaining warship from this period in London and one of only three anywhere in UK, in 2014 its hull was repainted in striking 'dazzle camouflage' by German artist Tobias Rehberger, as a centennial com-memoration of 'the Great War'. In 2016 HMS *President* was relocated temporarily for maintenance work.

This class of ship was named after flowers and saxifrage is a flower commonly found in London.

9. Animals

Unveiled in 2004, the stone and bronze 'Animals In War' memorial commemorates millions of creatures that served and perished alongside British and Allied servicemen and women. Horses, elephants, camels, dogs, oxen, carrier pigeons, mules, donkeys, cats – even glow-worms – are shown as if making the final journey from life to death. A poignant inscription reminds us that 'They had no choice'.

10. Peace

In 1985 during a time of fear of nuclear holocaust and Cold War tension, London's Peace Pagoda was constructed by a Japanese order of Buddhist monks and nuns promoting global harmony in the atomic age. This unique London landmark takes the form of a '*stupa*', a monumental structure contain-ing gilt-bronze statues of the Buddha. Battersea's riverside pagoda in its park setting has become a much-loved haven of tranquillity amidst the city's ceaseless hustle and bustle, as it invites each of us to stop and think about our world.

TOUR 8

Flora & Fauna

These questions invite you out on another tour of London's natural environment where we'll discover plants and animals with amazing stories.

1. What wild animals are found in large herds in Bushy Park and Richmond Park?

2. True or false? Winnie the Pooh was a bear who lived in London Zoo.

3. What commonly seen tree is a hybrid of Oriental and Western Planes (*P. orientalis* and *P. occidentalis*)?

4. Which of these animals is not part of the natural history of the Tower of London?

   a. Ravens
   b. Polar bear
   c. Elephant

   d. Lions
   e. Monkeys
   f. Black adder

5. What animal connects these famous London residents and venues?

   - Dr Samuel Johnson
   - Mayor Richard 'Dick' Whittington
   - 10 Downing Street
   - The Savoy Hotel

6. What is London Pride?

   a. Insect
   b. Grass
   c. Bird

   d. Flowering plant
   e. Variety of apple

7. In which London UNESCO World Heritage Site will you find giant Amazon waterlilies?

8. Which City livery companies conduct the annual census of swans on the Thames?

9. Which native bird from the Himalayas and Brazil has been colonising aggressively in London's parks and open spaces for fifty years?

10. What is Burlington House's unique connection with the naming of plants and animals?

After that tour we'll take a moment to enjoy some of London's 'creature comforts' before we head off once more.

Answers: Tour 8

1. Deer
Herds of red and fallow deer roam peacefully in these south London public parks on lands that once were royal hunting grounds.

2. True
Well, sort of true. Winnie (after Canadian town Winnipeg) was an orphaned bear cub brought to Europe by Lt Harry Colebourn during the First World War. The Canadian regimental mascot was left at the zoo for safe-keeping and became a popular attraction for Londoners during those war years, including author A.A. Milne and his son, Christopher Robin. And so was born the fictional bear 'Winnie the Pooh'. That's a fact Pooh's friend Eeyore could put in his 'Useful Pot'!

3. London Plane
Platanus × acerifola is a hybrid thought by some experts to have been discovered in the garden of seventeenth-century plant-collectors John Tradescant (father and son), who introduced many non-native species. London Plane trees were planted extensively during the eighteenth and nineteenth-century Industrial Revolution when London would have been full of soot and dirt. These trees proved excellent at absorbing pollutants and freshening the air, shedding excess carbon dioxide as bark. First plantings outside London date back to the 1660s; the oldest examples in town may be the youngsters in Berkeley Square W1 planted in 1789.

The Tradescants are buried in the Lambeth graveyard of a deconsecrated church now blooming anew as the Garden Museum.

4. f. Black adder

The adder or viper is Britain's only venomous native snake but don't worry, you will find Blackadder on TV or DVD as the central character in a popular BBC comedy series.

These other creatures lived at the Tower during its history as a palace and fortress, and ravens still live there. A guided tour explains the fascinating – and sometimes sad – stories of the creatures kept in London's royal keep.

5. Cat

Dr Johnson published his celebrated English dictionary in 1755 while living in Gough Square, EC4, where a statue of his beloved feline friend, Hodge, is located. Legend tells that Whittington (c. 1350–1423) became rich and famous thanks to the rat-catching skills of his cat. The Prime Minister's Downing Street residence is the purlieu of a cat known as 'Chief Mouser to the Cabinet Office'. Occupants of this top office include Humphrey (under PMs Thatcher, Major and Blair) and the current incumbent Larry. The Savoy Hotel's resident black cat is a small, wooden sculpture called 'Kaspar' (incidentally, carved from London Plane), who has a place laid at table in the event that thirteen people should wish to sit down to dine together. It may be superstitious but who would want to risk a ... catastrophe?

6. d. Flowering plant

Saxifraga × urbium is a small, perennial flower long popular in London. It acquired a special symbolism for Londoners because it regrew determinedly on bombsites during the Second World War. Celebrated composer Noel Coward wrote a haunting song in 1941 that strengthened this association. Nowadays it is also a popular brand of beer brewed by Fuller's in London.

7. Royal Botanic Gardens, Kew

Victoria amazonica, V. Longwood and *V. cruziana* are spectacular plants found in Kew's Princess of Wales Conservatory and Waterlily House. Leaves exceed 8ft in diameter, easily supporting the weight of a small child. Kew houses many beautiful displays of plants from around the world, and its extensive seed banks make a vital contribution to international research into conservation, medicine and farming.

8. Vintners and Dyers

Since medieval times these livery companies representing the wine and textile-dyeing trades have been granted the privilege of owning swans – then considered meat fit for the royal table. Swans were also a valuable source of writing quills and warm down. In July, a procession of small boats covers an upstream stretch of the Thames, auditing the swan population and checking their health. 'Swan-Upping' also divides ownership fairly between the sovereign and the two companies.

A central London statue of the Vintners' Swan Marker and Barge Master in ceremonial dress is an excellent jumping-off point for a tour about London's ancient trades and traditions.

9. Parakeet

Psittacula krameri is a brightly coloured non-native bird that is adapting surprisingly well to the English climate, to the extent that 50,000 may now be living in the wild, to the detriment of native species. Often a luminous green hue and with a piercing screech, there are several equally colourful tales about how their ancestors may have escaped into our open spaces – from the set of 1951 film *The African Queen* starring Humphrey Bogarde and Katharine Hepburn, or released by rock guitar legend Jimi Hendrix during his stay in London, or flying out of aviaries damaged during a storm in the late 1980s.

10. It is the home of the Linnean Society's specimen plant and animal collection, a primary reference for all taxonomy

The Society owns several important collections, including those of eighteenth-century Swedish scientist Carl von Linné (Linnaeus). His plants and animals were brought to London after his death by Sir James Edward Smith, himself the owner of an important shell and carpological collection. Because Linnaeus is credited with devising the binomial system used to name every single plant and creature, his collection is considered to be of primary importance for each and every *Homo sapiens*.

TOUR 9

Famous & Infamous

Now let's meet some of the women and men who have shaped London.

1. Which French refugee opened a revolutionary wax museum and Chamber of Horrors in the early nineteenth century?

2. Which influential German-born socialist philosopher moved to London in 1849?

3. Which medieval cloth merchant and mouse-botherer became Mayor on four occasions and left a valuable legacy to Londoners?

4. Which eighteenth-century American diplomat and scientist's house on Craven Street, WC2 is open to visitors?

5. In which London institution is the laboratory where Michael Faraday made world-changing discoveries that harnessed electric power?

6. Which pioneering nurse is commemorated by a statue on Waterloo Place, SW1?

7. Which Victorian social reformer is commemorated in a famous statue at Piccadilly Circus?

8. Name the first Governor of New South Wales, whose statue on Watling Street is near his birthplace.

9. What child welfare institution founded by Captain Thomas Coram benefitted from London's first public art gallery and the generosity of composer Handel?

10. What was invented by civil engineer James Greathead that enabled safe expansion of London's underground railways?

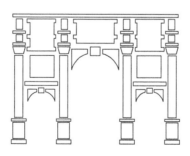

Well, did you make it through that round safely?
A pause for breath, then let's head off once more.

Answers: Tour 9

1. Marie Tussaud (1761-1850)
Mme Tussaud began producing wax death masks at the height of executions during the French Revolution. She established an attraction in London during the Napoleonic Wars that has grown into a global chain of wax museums showcasing the famous and infamous.

2. Karl Marx (1818-1883)
Marx's collaboration with Friedrich Engels began in Paris and Brussels. After the publication of *The Communist Manifesto* they moved to London, where his favourite workplace became the British Museum's Reading Room. *Das Kapital* influenced generations of political and economic revolutionaries. Visit his grave in Highgate Cemetery and find the blue plaque marking one of his family homes on Dean Street in Soho, W1.

3. Richard (Dick) Whittington (c. 1350-1423)
Legend relates the inspiring tale of this young man without an inheritance, who makes a fortune thanks to his cat – apparently an accomplished rodent-catcher – and a happy marriage to the boss's daughter.

In fact, mercer Whittington rose to prosperity through selling cloth and making loans to royalty and courtiers. Mayor on four occasions, he died childless, endowing his adoptive city with an impressive legacy of civic institutions.

After visiting Marx's grave, head down Highgate Hill to find a monument near Whittington Hospital, said to mark the spot where he (and his cat) heard church bells calling him to 'turn again' from early disappointment towards glittering success.

4. Benjamin Franklin (1706-90)

Occupied by Franklin for sixteen years, this is his only home that has survived in Britain or America. Here you will discover the life and times of a man at the forefront of events that were to separate Britain and its American colonies. Franklin also left an important scientific legacy.

5. The Royal Institution, Albemarle Street, W1

Michael Faraday (1791-1867) was mentored by Institution President Sir Humphry Davy, and his laboratory is the focus of displays celebrating the institution's wider scientific contribution. Here Faraday harnessed the latent power of electricity, inventing the modern motor, transformer, generator and dynamo.

The RI is just one of many sites in London to discover for yourself local landmarks in universal scientific progress.

6. Florence Nightingale (1820-1910)

Born in Florence, Italy, Nightingale trained as a nurse before being asked in 1854 by Secretary of War Lord Herbert of Lea (statue next to hers) to take a team of nurses to the Crimean battlefront. Appalled by rudimentary conditions and high mortality rates, Nightingale's caring, scientific approach significantly improved soldiers' medical care, saving many lives. Nightingale is depicted as 'the lady of the lamp' visiting wards at night. Returning home, she helped improve public medicine, while inspiring and training a corps of professional nurses fit for the world of modern medicine.

Follow the London trail of other pioneering medical women including Jamaican-born nurse Mary Seacole, physician Elizabeth Garrett Anderson and surgeon Dame Louisa Aldrich-Blake.

7. Lord Shaftesbury (1801-1885)

Shaftesbury was a politician and social reformer whose legacy includes improvements to industrial practices regulating child labour (e.g. boy chimney-sweeps), women's working conditions and treatment of the mentally ill. Shaftesbury was known as 'the poor man's earl'. A statue and fountain at this important road junction and the grand avenue directly north-east stand testament to his achievements.

Correctly called 'The Angel of Christian Charity' after Shaftesbury's sense of Christian duty, the statue is referred to popularly as 'Eros' (Greek god of erotic love), although knowledgeable guides patiently explain that it represents Anteros (Eros' half-brother, the god of selfless love).

8. Admiral Arthur Phillip (1738-1814)

During his career in the Royal Navy, Phillip was tasked by government minster Lord Sydney with leading the first expedition to colonise distant Australia. The First Fleet made landfall in 1788 near where the town of Sydney now stands. Phillip became first Governor of New South Wales and rose to the challenge of developing the new colony. The nearby church of St Mary le Bow contains other links to former colonies in Australia and Virginia.

9. The Foundling Hospital, Brunswick Square, WC1

Sea captain Coram (1668-1751) was shocked by the sight of abandoned, illegitimate children on the streets and established London's first children's charity. Granted a Royal Charter by King George II in 1739, the hospital eventually cared for 25,000 children before placing its last child in foster care in 1954. The Coram charity continues to help 1 million children around the country each year.

Part of the building now tells the remarkable history of this hospital's children and their mothers' social circumstances. Adults may only enter the adjacent Coram's Fields playground when accompanying a child.

George Frideric Handel launched the hospital's first celebrity fundraising concert in 1749 and organised an annual concert of his *Messiah*. Artist William Hogarth donated a painting as a raffle prize and encouraged contemporaries to support Britain's first free public art gallery. Later supporters included artists Thomas Gainsborough and Joshua Reynolds, as well as writer Charles Dickens.

10. The 'travelling shield'
Digging underground tunnels was hazardous work until South African-born engineer Greathead (1844-1896) perfected his hydraulic-propelled protective cage for miners. As Chief Engineer of the City & South London Railway (today part of the Northern line), his device for safer cutting of deep, metal-lined tunnels enabled electric trains to replace steam locomotives that ran in 'cut and cover' hand-dug trenches. This created London's 'Tube' network.

Remember to thank Greathead as you journey underground to enjoy London's sights. You'll find his statue disguising a station air vent by the Royal Exchange!

TOUR 10

Rivers & Waterways

The Thames defines London's landscape and shapes much of its history. Let's now cruise along the mighty river and explore tributaries, canals and waterways with interesting stories to tell.

1. Which of these rivers and streams is not in the London area?

   a. Neckinger
   b. Brent
   c. Mutton Brook
   d. Ching
   e. Cherwell
   f. Quaggy

2. Which bridge has granite piers decorated with images of freshwater birds upstream and sea birds downstream?

3. What engineering solution has protected central London from destructive tidal surges since 1982?

4. Which is the only London borough to straddle the Thames?

5. Which section of the Thames is known as the Upper Pool?

6. Which of London's 'lost waterways' passes under Holborn Viaduct?

7. Which river passes in a large pipe seen above the platforms at Sloane Square Tube station?

8. Why have there been no 'Frost Fairs' in central London since the early nineteenth century?

9. On which stretch of water will you find the Rolling Bridge, Helix Bridge and Fan Bridge?

10. On which river is the Mill House, believed to be the world's oldest existing tidal mill?

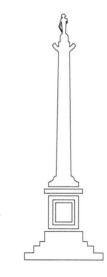

And now it's time to flow on to our next themed tour.

Answers: Tour 10

1. e. Cherwell

The Cherwell ('CHAR-well') is a tributary of the Thames near Oxford. You might be forgiven for thinking south-east London's Quaggy sounds Australian but these local waters flow into another tributary or into the Thames itself.

2. Blackfriars Bridge

Opened by Queen Victoria in 1869 to replace a century-old bridge, Blackfriars' capitals are decorated with birds and plants from the tidal Thames.

3. Thames Barrier

Straddling the Thames east of the city centre between Silvertown and New Charlton, this elegantly engineered system is designed to let shipping pass through, while ten steel gates lie on the riverbed ready to be raised when an exceptional surge of water arrives upriver from the North Sea. Longer than ten Olympic swimming pools, the world's second largest flood barrier is part of an integrated flood plan protecting 48 sq. miles of central London. The on-site information centre includes a working model.

When near the river, ask your guide to tell you about those often-overlooked lions' heads with metal rings in their mouths along the embankment in central London.

4. Richmond-upon-Thames

The clue is in the full name of this administrative district formed in 1965 from parts of Surrey and Middlesex. With 21 miles of river frontage, Richmond boasts several great royal or stately homes near London's watery highway, including Hampton Court Palace, Strawberry Hill, Marble Hill House and Kew Palace. The Royal Botanical Gardens at Kew and the London Wetlands Centre in Barnes are two natural treasures.

5. Tower of London – London Bridge

One of the world's busiest ports stretched right into the centre of London until the late twentieth century. Before enclosed docks and warehouses started to be built downriver at the turn of the nineteenth century, sailing ships unloaded cargo from moorings in the river onto small boats ('lighters') or directly onto riverside wharves and the Legal Quays in the Pool of London, especially in the Upper Pool. Tower Bridge was designed in the late nineteenth century with a roadway that raises to let through shipping.

6. Fleet River

One of three notable 'lost rivers' rising in north London, the Fleet was an important waterway until covered over after becoming unsanitary. Unseen, it still flows in a culvert under Farringdon Street through its ancient valley, spanned by Holborn Viaduct, before entering the Thames under Blackfriars Bridge. Queen Victoria opened the bridge and viaduct on the same day in 1869. London's famous 'street of ink', Fleet Street, flows west from the valley.

7. Westbourne

The second of those 'lost rivers', the Westbourne rises on Hampstead Heath and flows in underground sewer pipes until it emerges on Chelsea Embankment. It was at one time crossed by a 'knight's bridge', the origin of that district's name.

Keen to detect the third 'lost river'? Ask your guide to show you a small section of the Tyburn flowing through the basement of an antiques centre near Bond Street in an open channel stocked with golden fish, before entering the Thames at an outfall near Vauxhall Bridge. A fishy fact, indeed!

8. The Thames became faster-flowing

Faster because the tidal river had been made narrower through land reclamation; the arches of John Rennie's newly built London Bridge in the 1820s were wider than its predecessor; and temperatures were rising again after the end of a 'Little Age Ice' across Europe. Without ice-sheets forming or ice-blocks trapped under the arches, there was no solid surface for stalls and fun-fairs that had been popular since the seventeenth century.

To see a depiction of 'Frost Fairs', ask your guide to point out ceramic panels on the southern riverside walkway under Southwark Bridge.

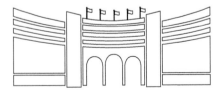

9. Paddington Basin on the Paddington Arm of the Grand Junction and Regent's Canal system

Near Isambard Kingdom Brunel's magnificent Paddington terminus built for the Great Western Railway runs a nineteenth-century waterway connecting London's docks with the country's inland manufacturing and commodities centres. An offshoot of Britain's extensive canal system near 'Little Venice', Paddington Basin is no longer used industrially and is being regenerated as a corporate and residential quarter. Pedestrian and cycle paths border the canal, and 'artwork bridges' have been commissioned from noted designers to provide improved access and add a touch of delight. These bridges at intervals turn like a corkscrew, or in a splayed motion, or unfurl. This all makes for a very moving sight!

10. River Lea

The present building in Bromley-by-Bow dates from 1776, although there was a watermill recorded here even earlier than the eleventh-century Domesday Book. Harnessing a strong tidal flow along this important Thames tributary, the mill was used to grind grain for flour and, later, gin production. A continuing project is raising funds to restore machinery and conserve this important piece of east London's industrial heritage.

A visitor information centre offers an introduction to the mill and the area around the Queen Elizabeth Olympic Park.

TOUR 11

Ceremony & Pageantry

London is renowned for its brilliant royal pageants and traditional ceremonial events. This tour will give us plenty of colourful sights to enjoy!

1. Match these personnel to the customary location of their ceremonial duties:

    a. Queen's Foot Guards   i. Houses of Parliament
    b. Household Cavalry   ii. Buckingham Palace
    c. Yeoman Warder   iii. Guildhall
    d. Black Rod   iv. Horseguards
    e. Swordbearer of London   v. Tower of London

2. Which crown does the sovereign wear at the State Opening of Parliament and at the end of the coronation service?

3. What type of ceremonial vehicle was made by Giovanni Baptista Cipriani for the Lord Mayor in 1757 and by W.J. Frecklington for the Queen in 1988?

4. Where does Europe's largest street carnival take place each year in August?

5. Name the military parade held in June to celebrate the sovereign's official birthday.

6. Name the public parade held in November when the new Lord Mayor of the City of London is presented to citizens.

7. What noisy ceremonial events are carried out at the Tower of London by the Honourable Artillery Company and in Green Park by the King's Troop Royal Horse Artillery?

8. What ceremony is commemorated in the name of the Smithfield pub, The Hand & Shears?

9. Name the institution on Queen Victoria Street, EC4 that advises on all aspects of public ceremony.

10. Name the royal boat launched in 2012 to celebrate Queen Elizabeth II's Diamond Jubilee.

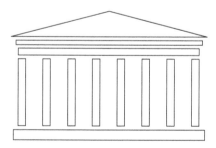

There are many more great ceremonies to enjoy during your time in London, but time marches on and we're off to explore the sounds of London.

Answers: Tour 11

1. a. – ii; b. – iv; c. – v; d. – i; e. – iii

The Household Division is formed of seven regiments of operational soldiers. Five foot guard regiments wear scarlet tunics and black bearskin caps, two cavalry regiments respectively wear red or blue tunics, shiny metal breastplates and plumed helmets. Guard changes at Buckingham Palace and Horse Guards are 'must see' ceremonies.

Yeoman Warders, better known as 'Beefeaters', started as fifteenth-century royal bodyguards. Their descendants help look after the Tower of London and attend the sovereign on ceremonial occasions.

A security officer responsible for order in the House of Lords, The Gentleman Usher of the Black Rod's role includes summoning members of the Commons to hear the Queen's Speech during Official Opening of the new parliamentary session – at which time the Commons' door is pointedly slammed in their face to demonstrate MPs' independence. Ouch!

The Swordbearer of London accompanies the Lord Mayor of London on civic duties bearing their sword. The Swordbearer manages the mayor's daily schedule. In a pocket inside their fur hat is kept the key to a box containing one of the city's official seals.

2. Imperial State Crown

One of the highlights in the Crown Jewels, the Imperial State Crown is kept on public display in the Tower of London when not in use. This magnificent crown includes a flawless 317 carat diamond known as the 'Second Star of Africa', the Black Prince's Ruby, the Stuart Sapphire, St Edward's Sapphire and Queen Elizabeth I's Pearls.

3. A horse-drawn coach

The Lord Mayor's ceremonial coach decorated by Italian-born painter Cipriani spends most of the year in the Museum of London. Frecklington's Australian State Coach was a high-tech gift from the Australian people celebrating their country's bicentenary in 1988 and is kept on display in the Royal Mews at Buckingham Palace.

4. Notting Hill

Originating in London's Caribbean communities during the 1960s, this street carnival has blossomed into the world's second largest with 1 million people participating or attending. Enjoy the parade of colourful and often noisy floats, masquerades, sound systems, steel pan bands, calypso, soca and tasty delights influenced by French, Spanish, Dutch, British and African cuisine, such as jerk chicken, roti or curried goat.

5. Trooping the Colour

Attended by the sovereign, senior members of the Royal Family, invited guests and members of the public, this splendid ceremony takes place on Horseguards Parade during what should be fine, summer weather. All seven regiments of the Household Division parade their regimental flags ('colours'), with their bands adding a rousing soundtrack to the occasion. Members of the public line the vicinity or watch on television. Preparatory rehearsals can be a pleasant surprise during walking tours through the royal district.

6. Lord Mayor's Show

Riding in the magnificent eighteenth-century horse-drawn coach at the head of a long and colourful parade celebrating the City's communities, traditions and activities, the incoming Lord Mayor processes to Westminster to swear a formal oath of allegiance to the sovereign. After the parade, the day's events include walks led by City of London guides for members of the public to explore the City, and a spectacular fireworks show on the river.

7. Gun salutes

Salutes mark royal birthdays, anniversaries, national events and visits by Heads of State. Depending on occasion and location, 21–124 rounds are fired. City-based HAC has the honour of firing salutes at the Tower of London, and the Troop brings horse-drawn gun carriages to salutes in Royal Parks.

8. The Lord Mayor cutting a ribbon or piece of cloth to declare the annual cloth fair open

From 1133, the priory of St Bartholomew held a fair in August around the feast day of its saint. This useful income stream grew into England's leading cloth market, as well as Londoners' favourite funfest. From the seventeenth century after coming under City authority, the event would be opened by the Lord Mayor formally cutting a piece of material or snipping a ribbon in front of this tavern where cloth merchants were based during the fair.

9. College of Arms (or Heralds' College)

Created in 1484 and headed by the Earl Marshal, this is the official heraldic authority for England, Wales, Northern

Ireland and much of the Commonwealth including Australia and New Zealand. Heralds are responsible for the granting of new coats of arms and maintain registers of arms, pedigrees, genealogies, Royal Licences, changes of name, and flags. They advise on all matters relating to ceremony, the peerage and baronetage, precedence and honours, as well as national and community symbols including flags.

10. The Queen's Rowbarge *Gloriana*

The first royal rowbarge built in 250 years, *Gloriana* is bigger than her predecessors and needs the combined effort of eighteen burly oarsmen to glide along the Thames – the principal route for royal and civic processions through London's history. After starring in the unforgettable 670-boat Thames Diamond Jubilee Pageant in 2012, *Gloriana* is providing opportunities for charities to participate in special events on London's great waterway, helping to promote the river's use and encouraging young people to take up rowing.

Watch out for this gilded beauty during your tours near the river.

TOUR 12

Music & Song

Everyone loves a good tune, so let's now hear some of London's musical stories and see where it all goes on.

1. Outside which recording studios is the road-crossing immortalised on the cover of an album by The Beatles?

2. Name the annual concert series started in 1895 and based in the Royal Albert Hall.

3. Which enormous, brown-brick building features on the cover of rock band Pink Floyd's 1977 album *Animals*?

4. With which district of inner London is singer Amy Winehouse most associated?

5. At which venue was Michael Jackson booked for a fifty-night residency in 2009?

6. Which concert hall on Waterloo's South Bank was built for the 1951 Festival of Britain?

7. In which south London district is *Electric Avenue*?

8. Which Croydon performing arts college trained international pop star Adele?

9. Which German-born, London-based composer's suite was premiered in 1717 on the Thames for the pleasure of German-born, German-based King George I?

10. What distinctive form of musical entertainment takes place at Wilton's in the East End?

Our next movement looks at London's sports and leisure activities.

Answers: Tour 12

1. Abbey Road Studios

EMI's studios on Abbey Road in St John's Wood, NW8 have been in use for classical, choral and pop music recordings since 1931. Several Beatles albums were produced here by (Sir) George Martin and *Abbey Road* was to be their last recording (and second-to-last release) before splitting up.

Considered one of the greatest pop music albums, its 1969 cover photo of George, bare-footed Paul, Ringo and John on a striped 'zebra crossing' is still re-enacted by fans visiting from all over the world. Just don't tell them that the crossing has been relocated from its original location!

2. Henry Wood Promenade Concerts ('The Proms')

Named after its founder, since the 1940s the Proms have been performed in Kensington's 6,000-seat Royal Albert Hall – built with profits from the 1851 Great Exhibition Albert had promoted, and named in turn after Queen Victoria's deceased husband. Today, the varied programme extends to 100 concerts over an 8-week summer season, and has been called the 'largest and most democratic' classical music festival in the world. The 'Last Night of the Proms' is a much-loved national institution that includes a mass singalong to *Land of Hope and Glory* and *Rule, Britannia*.

There are musical and cultural events year-round and opportunities to tour its grand interior. Feel free to hum a jaunty tune.

3. Battersea Power Station

Designed by Sir Giles Gilbert Scott as an electricity generating station, the towers of this riverside giant are a landmark. Disaster struck the British band's album cover shoot when a large, pink pig-shaped inflatable balloon came adrift from its mooring and floated languidly – and dangerously – over London's flightpaths. The former power station and surrounding district are undergoing major redevelopment as a new residential and diplomatic quarter.

Explore now and see tomorrow's London today.

4. Camden Town

Born in the outer suburb of Southgate, by the time of her premature death in 2011, Amy had moved to the inner-London borough of Camden for its boho, edgy vibe. Amy rose to prominence aged 16 as a jazz vocalist, before developing an award-winning international career that spanned jazz, R&B, soul, hip-hop and pop. Her best-selling records include *Back to Black*, *Valerie* and *Rehab*. Find sites associated with Amy's career around Camden and across town.

5. The O2 in Greenwich

At the time of his death, 'King of Pop' Jackson was rehearsing for a marathon residency at the world's top-grossing indoor music venue; 1 million tickets had been sold.

6. Royal Festival Hall

Originally part of a complex created in 1951 for a post-war festival to restore the nation's spirits and commemorate the centenary of 1851's Great Exhibition, the 2,500-seater hall is now a leading international performance venue in the

Southbank Centre. Waterloo's South Bank is one of London's premier cultural quarters, offering a wide mix of music, film, theatre, modern dance, poetry, performance and art.

7. Brixton

The title of the 1982 international hit by Guyanese–British singer Eddie Grant references a local shopping street that in 1880 became the first in the area to be lit by electricity. The song contrasts the gritty side of life there with its energising buzz. Famous for its bustling street market with flavours from the Caribbean, India, Asia, Africa, South America and Europe, Brixton is one of the most culturally diverse and creative areas of London. Venues including O2 Brixton Academy are popular for African and Caribbean music.

8. BRIT School for Performing Arts and Technology

With an A-list of alumni including music stars Leona Lewis, Jessie J, Katie Melua and Rizzle Kicks, BRIT is an incubator of British talent in the performing arts and performance technologies. The school nurtured husky-voiced, Tottenham-born chanteuse Adele (Adkins), whose second album *21* sold 30 million copies and topped charts around the world in 2011–12. Adele won an Oscar for singing the title-song of the Bond film *Skyfall*, and her hotly awaited follow-up album *25* was released in 2015.

Croydon is ready and waiting for *Someone Like You*.

9. Handel's *Water Music*

London's classical and choral musical tradition owes much to German-born composer George Frideric Handel, who settled in London as Britain's new Hanoverian (German) royal dynasty was dropping anchor. German-speaking King George I spoke little English and was said to prefer his native land to his new kingdom. However, during a river pageant he expressed his pleasure at Handel's latest composition by insisting it be played several more times by an orchestra of musicians teetering on barges.

Handel's home for thirty-six years on Brook Street W1 gives an insight into the composer's life and times. When you visit, you'll receive an 'Encore!' in the form of a blue plaque on the neighbouring house recording the 1960s residence of a very different musician – American rock-guitar legend Jimi Hendrix, whose restored 1960s flat is part of the newly opened 'Handel and Hendrix in London' museum. An unlikely duet, indeed!

10. Music hall variety shows

Wilton's Music Hall in Graces Alley, E1 (between Wapping and Whitechapel) is a rare survivor of a once commonplace venue for popular musical entertainment. Usually connected with taverns or public houses, between the 1850s–1881 Wilton's operated as a music hall offering a varied programme of popular song, dance and bawdy entertainment for ordinary local residents, incoming sailors and merchants in the East End docks. For its often struggling clientele, the flashy building was an attraction in its own right: mirrors, chandeliers, painted décor, warmth, light, ventilation.

Imaginatively conserved and modernised, Wilton's reopened recently to gain a new lease of life. To visit this music hall is to step back in time.

TOUR 13

Sport & Leisure

Sport is a big part of Londoners' interests, either taking part or as spectators. Now it's time to get our muscles warmed up before taking a gentle jog around the local sports scene.

1. Match these British sports stars to their respective London stadia or sports venue:

   a. Booby Moore, David Beckham
   b. W.G. Grace, James Anderson
   c. Virginia Wade, Andy Murray
   d. Jessica Ennis-Hill, Mo Farah
   e. Dame Sarah Storey, Sir Chris Hoy
   f. Jonny Wilkinson, Jason Robinson

   i. Twickenham
   ii. Lord's
   iii. The Stadium, Olympic Park
   iv. Velodrome, Olympic Park
   v. Wimbledon
   vi. Wembley

2. Which long-distance foot-race has taken place in London annually since 1981? It covers a scenic route from Blackheath to Buckingham Palace.

3. Which of these professional sports is not regularly played professionally at Wembley Stadium?

   a. Football
   b. Rugby League
   c. American Football
   d. Baseball

4. What frosty fun is enjoyed year-round at venues in Bayswater, Lea Valley and Alexandra Palace, and winter pop-up locations including the moat at the Tower of London, Canary Wharf and Somerset House?

5. During London 2012, which Olympic sports competition was held on the Horse Guards parade ground in Whitehall?

6. Which rowing race has the longest course: Oxford–Cambridge Boat Race or Doggett's Coat & Badge Race?

7. In which of these sports is GB's representative, the City of London Police Force team, still officially the Olympic champion?

   a. Deck quoits
   b. Longbow archery
   c. Jousting
   d. Fencing
   e. Tug-of-war
   f. Tossing the truncheon

8. What cerebral game's twelfth-century pieces found on the Isle of Lewis are on display in London at the British Museum?

9. The largest park in central London has 5 miles of bridleways and a manège for horse-riding lessons, jumping and dressage. What is its name?

10. With what sport do you associate London-born eighteenth-century world champion Daniel Mendoza, whose technique transformed his sport?

   A knockout ending to your sporting tour of London!

Answers: Tour 13

1. a. – vii, Football
    b. – ii, Cricket
    c. – vi, Tennis
    d. – iv, Track & Field Athletics
    e. – v, Cycling
    f. – i, Rugby Union

2. The London Marathon

This 26-mile, 365-yard Spring challenge includes competitions for elite female and male athletes, and a public race with participants running in wacky costumes to raise money for charities – £800 million since 1981. The 2016 race received 274,000 applications.

3. d. Baseball

Rebuilt in 2007, 90,000-seater Wembley is home to England's national football team and hosts finals of major domestic and international competitions. Its excellent playing surface, facilities and broadcast infrastructure attract league matches of both rugby codes. American Football has grown in popularity with three regular season NFL games played here in London. However, baseball is yet to make it to first base.

4. Ice-skating

5. Beach Volleyball

Incongruous or inspired? Games organisers chose this gravel-covered military parade ground as the site for the beach volleyball competition. 2,274 tonnes of locally sourced sand was brought in for the courts and later recycled to create thirty-five courts throughout London.

6. Doggett's Coat & Badge Race

The world's oldest continuously raced rowing competition is also London's longest rowing course. Solo oarsmen beginning careers as river watermen first raced in 1715 over a 4.5-mile course from London Bridge–Cadogan Pier. The winner was awarded a scarlet jacket and silver badge by theatre manager Thomas Doggett. Its 300th race in August 2015 was keenly contested, although watermen are not as numerous these days.

One of the world's most famous sporting contests is, simply, 'The Boat Race'. Male and female students at the universities of Oxford and Cambridge race in eights along a 4-mile 374-yard course from Putney–Mortlake. Look for concrete posts on the south bank inscribed 'UBR'. This great race has been keenly contested since 1829, moving later to this section of the lower Thames where it draws large crowds each spring and millions of TV viewers worldwide.

7. e. Tug-of-war

Seriously, I am not pulling your leg! Tug-of-war was contested at five Summer Olympiads between 1900-20. At the 1908 London Games, GB entered three teams with the City of London Police team winning Gold, the Metropolitan Police winning Silver and the Liverpool Police bagging Bronze. Home team advantage?

In 1912 in Stockholm, the home team beat the City of London Police (representing GB) in the final and in 1920 the City force again won Gold in the next Games in Paris. In its infinite wisdom, the International Olympic Committee (IOC) then removed the Tug-of-war and numerous other 'sports' from its bloated programme, meaning that, technically, the City's sturdy force remains Olympic champion!

8. Chess

Debates rage as to whether chess is a game or a sport – it is on IOC's official list and was an Exhibition Sport at Sydney 2000 – but there is no debate about the beauty of the 'Lewis Chessmen', a collection of intricately carved walrus ivory and whales' teeth pieces made in Scandinavia in the twelfth century and found on a Scottish island 800 years later.

Chess fans may also care to check out historic restaurant Simpsons-in-the-Strand, opened in 1828 as a chess club and coffee house.

9. Hyde Park

A popular venue between the sixteenth and early twentieth centuries for fashionable promenading on horseback or in swanky, horse-drawn carriages, 340-acre Hyde Park is still the preferred city centre exercise ground for recreational, military and police horse-riding. There are public stables nearby where riders of all abilities may hire horses or ponies.

So, how about an unforgettable tour of Hyde Park – on horseback?

10. Boxing

East End-born Mendoza (1764-1836) was a bare-knuckle boxer in the days before modern rules. This fighter overcame physical disadvantages (height 5ft 7in, weight 160lb) and avoided scrappy mauling by application of his 'scientific method' that outsmarted chunkier opponents. His reliance on rapid, rather than hard punching, and on physical fitness, courage and an agile, dancing style are standard today. Mendoza is celebrated as the first Jewish world champion and was feted nationally in his lifetime, especially after publishing his influential book *The Art of Boxing* in 1795.

'Mendoza the Jew's' Bethnal Green house is marked by a blue plaque, and his burial place in Nuevo Cemetery, on a university campus in Mile End, is commemorated by a plaque.

TOUR 14

Religion & Worship

As a multi-cultural city for much of its history, Londoners follow many different religions – or none at all – and many striking buildings will be seen on every tour. Let's explore this heritage.

1. Match up these religious denominations with an example of their local centre of worship:

    a. Anglican
    b. Roman Catholic
    c. Methodist
    d. Sikh

    e. Muslim
    f. Jewish
    g. Russian Orthodox
    h. Hindu

    i. Westminster Cathedral
    ii. Bevis-Marks Synagogue, City of London
    iii. BAPS Shri Swaminarayan Mandir, Neasden
    iv. Khalsa Jatha Gurdwara, Shepherd's Bush
    v. Westminster Abbey
    vi. Cathedral of the Dormition of the Mother of God & The Royal Martyrs, Chiswick
    vii. London Central Mosque, Regent's Park
    viii. Central Hall, Westminster

2. Name the Archbishop of Canterbury's London residence.

3. Which one of these churches is not the work of Sir Christopher Wren?

    a. St Paul's Cathedral
    b. St James, Piccadilly
    c. Chapel of the Royal Hospital, Chelsea

    d. St Stephen Walbrook
    e. All Hallows-by-the-Tower

4. Which east London company made Westminster's most famous bell and many other church bells for this country and around the English-speaking world?

5. Which pupil of Wren designed these beautiful baroque churches?

   > Christ Church, Spitalfields; St George's, Bloomsbury; St Alphege, Greenwich; St Mary Woolnoth, City of London; West Towers of Westminster Abbey

6. To which saint is dedicated the great twelfth-century Gothic church in Smithfield?

7. What is unique about the chapel on the corner of Fournier Street and Brick Lane in Spitalfields built by French Protestant refugees in 1743?

8. By which name is the Church of St Saviour and St Mary Overie commonly known today?

9. Which small church forms part of the UNESCO World Heritage Site in Westminster?

10. Which City church that reopened after a 1993 bombing has a non-denominational Centre for Reconciliation and Peace?

A peaceful note on which to end our spiritual journey.

Answers: Tour 14

1. a. – v
    b. – i
    c. – viii
    d. – iv
    e. – vii
    f. – ii
    g. – vi
    h. – iii

2. Lambeth Palace

Across the river from the royal and governmental quarter is the residence of the spiritual head of the Church of England. Dating back nearly 800 years, the palace has witnessed the national church's journey from Catholic to Protestant faith – a story explained during a visit inside these ancient walls.

3. e. All Hallows-by-the-Tower

'Wrenaissance' churches sometimes seem to be everywhere, with his office involved in rebuilding fifty-one City churches and one cathedral after the Great Fire of 1666, as well as new places of worship in other districts. However, All Hallows lies to the east of the fire's destructive path and did not require his professional attention.

4. Whitechapel Bell Foundry

Britain's oldest manufacturing company began making bells in 1570. Its output includes Philadelphia's Liberty Bell (1752), the Great Bell of Montreal (1843) and a 13.5-tonne bell for the new Houses of Parliament bell tower in Westminster (1858), the largest bell ever cast in the foundry.

5. Nicholas Hawksmoor

Hawksmoor designed monumental new landmarks to promote the Church of England to London's increasingly diverse or faithless communities. His distinctive designs for spires also helped everyone navigate through the fast-expanding metropolis. Often overshadowed by other contemporary architects, his surviving churches are now appreciated for refining a uniquely English baroque style.

6. St Bartholomew

Twelfth-century monk and courtier Rahere founded the priory church of St Bartholomew the Great after an inspirational vision of the saint, whose statue and martyr's attribute (flaying knife) may be seen above a timber-framed gateway into the now-reduced precincts. You may even recognise the atmospheric interior of this beautiful parish church as it is often used as a location for TV and film productions.

7. It is the only building in Britain (some say outside Israel) that has been a centre of worship for three Abrahamic religions: Christianity, Judaism and Islam.

Founded in 1743 as La Neuve Eglise by Huguenots, whose presence in Spitalfields was later replaced by Jews, the building was converted into the Machzike Hadass synagogue in the 1860s. In turn, in the late twentieth century as the Jewish community moved on, Muslims from the Indian sub-continent, Africa and south-eastern Europe moved in and the building was re-converted into its present incarnation as the Jamme Masjid mosque.

Ask your guide to show you the poignantly prophetic inscription on a sundial on the Fournier Street side of this building.

8. Southwark Cathedral (more accurately 'The Cathedral and Collegiate Church of St Saviour and St Mary Overie, Southwark')

A church has existed for 1,400 years on this site in Borough close to the southern approach to London Bridge. The parish church of St Mary Overie ('over the river') was renamed St Saviour's in the sixteenth century after the split with Roman Catholicism. It was in the diocese of Winchester until the nineteenth-century population growth led to the creation of the diocese of Southwark.

9. St Margaret's

Identifiable today as 'the one with the circular, blue clock-face' immediately next to the great spiritual centre of Westminster Abbey, St Margaret's was established by Benedictine monks in the late eleventh century as a parish church specifically for local congregants. The two churches maintain a close working relationship and are 'royal peculiars' - outside formal authority of both the Bishop of London and the Archbishop of Canterbury - reporting directly to the Queen. Notable associations include William Caxton, fifteenth-century owner of England's first printing press, and sixteenth-century explorer Sir Walter Raleigh (both buried here), as well as Clementine Hozier and Winston Churchill, who were married here in 1908.

In addition to their architectural importance, the Palace of Westminster, Abbey and St Margaret's represent a long tradition of modern parliamentary monarchy and the development of influential parliamentary and constitutional institutions.

10. St Ethelburga-the-Virgin within Bishopsgate

Named after a seventh-century Saxon abbess of a Catholic convent, this small Anglican church was badly damaged by an IRA explosion targeting the surrounding business district. The fabric has been rebuilt and its ministry restored to include space for an innovative, non-profit charity that seeks to facilitate positive relationships bridging political, cultural or religious differences. Check out The Tent, an unusual sixteen-sided meeting space covered in fabric woven from goat's hair in Saudi Arabia and with windows spelling out 'Peace' in seven languages.

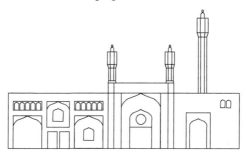

Food & Drink

Still hungry for more great experiences? Let's tuck in to some tasty food and drinks.

1. What combination of foods was made popular by young London restaurant entrepreneur Joseph Malin in the 1860s?

2. In which royal palace will you see working Tudor kitchens dating from the early sixteenth century, as well as the world's largest grape vine?

3. Which nineteenth-century businessman gave a collection of British art to a new gallery after making a fortune from sugar?

4. What tasty drink was developed by a doctor whose collection of curiosities helped create The British Museum?

5. Which food or drink became a hot success in London thanks to a new establishment opened by Pasqua Rosée in 1652?

6. Match these historic restaurants with their characteristic cuisine or signature dishes:

a. Simpson's Tavern,
   Ball Court Alley (1757)
b. Veeraswamy,
   Regent Street (1926)
c. Wilton's,
   Jermyn Street (1742)
d. Rules,
   Maiden Lane (1798)

i.   Game
ii. Oysters, fish, seafood
iii. Indian
iv. Meat chops, steak
     and similar fare

7. Which nineteenth-century architect is associated with the beautiful food-market buildings at Smithfield (London's main meat market), Billingsgate (fish) and Leadenhall (cheese, flowers and meat)?

8. Which brand of meat extract is cunningly – and permanently – advertised in an art deco tower prominent on the South Bank riverside?

9. Which London district became known as 'Biscuit Town' during the nineteenth and twentieth centuries?

10. Which north London museum tells the story of 'penny licks', a popular and affordable ice cream pioneered in nineteenth-century London by the Swiss-Italian Gatti family?

Didn't that taste good? We'll make time for a refreshment break before we head off on another tour that should suit you.

Answers: Tour 15

1. Fish and chips

Serving fried fish (traditional Jewish dish) with fried potatoes (introduced from Belgium or France) as a complete meal is believed to have been introduced by Malin's fish and chip shop in London's East End. Who was first is fiercely disputed – there is evidence of a fish and chip shop near Manchester around the same time – but there is no dispute that this tasty combination became the meal deal that defined British cuisine. A personal tip: instead of batter, for a crunchier texture try your fish fried in matzo crumbs (a special Jewish bread).

2. Hampton Court Palace

Huge kitchens that fed 600 people twice a day during King Henry VIII's reign are used today by historical chefs to prepare Tudor meals and demonstrate historic cooking techniques. Then head into the palace's gardens to find 'The Great Vine' (*Vitis vinifera Shiva Grossa* – Black Hamburg) planted in 1769 by renowned gardener Lancelot 'Capability' Brown. This venerable vine typically yields 600lb of grapes which are sold in September.

3. Sir Henry Tate

This successful tycoon behind Tate & Lyle created the Tate Gallery to display his collection of British art. The public gallery has built a collection that today numbers in excess of 70,000 items, resulting in expansion to four sites around England, two of which are in London – Tate Britain on Millbank in Chelsea and Tate Modern along the river on Bankside in central London. The Tate to Tate river boat service conveniently connects the two galleries.

4. Milk chocolate

Sir Hans Sloane was a doctor and collector of curiosities, who arranged for his immense collection to be acquired for display in a new 'British Museum' – the world's first free national public museum when founded in 1753. Working in the West Indies, Dr Sloane's experimental treatments included a chocolate drink that substituted the customary water, spices and sugar with sweetened cocoa beans boiled directly in milk. This gave a more pleasant taste and made a soothing treatment for patients suffering from indigestion or other ailments. On returning to England, his milk chocolate drink became popular and the recipe later passed to the Cadbury family of chocolatiers.

5. Coffee

In 1652, English merchant Daniel Edwards set up his Greek servant in business 'at the sign of Pasqua Rosée's head' in a City churchyard. From the grounds of this original coffee-house, the hot, new, dark brew became an instant success. Different coffeehouses began attracting people in specific lines of business or activity (cultural, political etc.), helping stimulate London's modern financial and commercial institutions, e.g. a coffeehouse opened in 1688 became the meeting point for merchants and financiers, who developed commercial insurance. Edward Lloyd's coffeehouse is long gone, while Lloyd's of London has grown into one of the world's insurance powerhouses.

A blue plaque off Cornhill, EC3 marks the site of this first stirring of London's business revolution.

6. a. – iv; b. – iii; c. – ii; d. – i

Simpson's Tavern is a City chophouse. It is the legacy of a format of dining dating to the late seventeenth century; meat remains the staple fare. Chophouses were succeeded by new styles of food and dining from continental Europe.

Veeraswamy is notable as the oldest surviving restaurant in London serving Indian cuisine, which reportedly has become the most popular style of cuisine in the UK.

Wilton's specialises in London's traditional street food – oysters, cockles and whelks – as well as other seafood and classic British fare.

Rules is highly regarded for seasonal game, as well as year-round classic British cuisine.

7. Sir Horace Jones

Jones was appointed Architect and Surveyor to the City in 1864 until his death in 1887. His legacy includes not only these three historic markets, but also Temple Bar marking the City's western border on Fleet Street, and the exterior of Tower Bridge.

8. Oxo

The Liebig Extract of Meat Company's riverside meat-processing factory was extended in the late 1920s with a tower in contemporary art deco style. Stamford Wharf was London's second highest commercial building, a feature exploited by the company's architect in circular and cross-shaped windows spelling out the name of their best-selling brand – and cunningly side-stepping inconvenient advertising restrictions. Take stock – today the renamed OXO Tower contains work spaces for local arts and crafts workers, along with places to eat and drink while enjoying views over the City.

9. Bermondsey

Extending inland south of Tower Bridge and the former docks of the Pool of London, Bermondsey became a major centre of biscuit production. This tasty tradition came to epitomise English tea-time. In the mid-nineteenth century Peek Frean's factory pioneered crumbly, sweet biscuits such as Bourbon, Marie, Custard Creams and Garibaldi (named after the charismatic Italian independence leader). This successful company later brought out savoury baked snacks, such as Twiglets and Cheeselets.

While Londoners developed a sweet tooth (and added a bit of weight around their waists), their pets benefitted from the expertise of Spiller's, whose bakers switched from supplying hard ship's biscuits for sea-dogs to hard biscuits for dogs and other animals.

10. London Canal Museum, New Wharf Road, N1

Carlo Gatti built an ice-house at Battle Bridge Basin on Regent's Canal in the 1860s to store ice imported from as far away as Norway, that ensured his supply of a key ingredient for ice creams. These were popular in his family's growing chain of affordable restaurants and sold on the streets for just a pre-decimal penny (1*d*). The site houses an interesting museum about Britain's extensive canal system and horse-drawn narrowboats that transported heavy cargo until the advent of railways.

TOUR 16

Design & Fashion

London's designers, labels, retailers, stylists, and models are cutting-edge, and London Fashion Week is a 'must-attend' event. Let's mooch off stylishly, discovering the people and places behind the styles, sales and celebrity stories.

1. Which West End street is famous for bespoke tailoring, especially gentlemen's suits?

2. Which East End district developed as a centre of silk-weaving and brocade production in the early eighteenth century?

3. The statue of which Regency dandy stands on Jermyn Street, SW1?

4. The home of which mid-nineteenth-century Arts & Crafts designer and manufacturer may be visited in Walthamstow, E17?

5. Which museum opened by Sir Terence Conran showcases the best of international design?

6. To which former medieval palace in south-east London did members of the Courtauld dynasty of thread and fabric manufacturers stitch on an art deco wing?

7. Match these London-based contemporary designers with their signature fashion item or style:

a. Victoria Beckham
b. Ozwald Boateng
c. Vivienne Westwood
d. Tomasz Starzewski
e. Sarah Burton
f. Philip Treacy
g. Anya Hindmarch
h. Jimmy Choo

i. Kate Middleton's wedding dress
ii. Shoes
iii. Men's tailoring with a twist
iv. Hats
v. Embroidery
vi. Bags and accessories
vii. Punks, pirates, Madame de Pompadour
viii. WAG fashion, 'His 'n' hers', wearability

8. True or false? A nineteenth-century hat designed in London to protect gamekeepers became a lethal projectile in the hands of henchman 'Oddjob' in the James Bond spy film *Goldfinger*.

9. Which Notting Hill museum displays a world-class collection of consumer advertising and brand ephemera?

10. Which fashion photographer and female model from the 'Swinging Sixties' are immortalised together in a bronze composition outside his former Mayfair studio?

Time perhaps to try on just one more pair of those little shoes, before we wear out more shoe-leather pounding the pavements on our next tour.

Answers: Tour 16

1. Savile Row, W1
Laid out 200 years ago as an elegant Mayfair street, by the mid-nineteenth century Savile Row had acquired a reputation as the place to go for bespoke tailoring, an international stature it defends fiercely. Tailors based here for more than 100 years are joined by newcomers to continue advancing London's reputation as a contemporary fashion leader.

2. Spitalfields, E1
French Huguenot refugees arriving after 1685 brought practical skills, including silk-weaving and fabric design. These talented craftsmen and women, who designed a practical style of terraced housing with well-lit attics for their looms, went on to build a reputation for top-quality decorative and dress fabrics. The eighteenth-century English designer Anna-Maria Garthwaite moved here for that reason. Find her blue-plaqued house on Princelet Street and examples of her silk brocade work in South Kensington's V&A Museum.

3. George 'Beau' Brummell (1788-1840)
'*To be truly elegant one should not be noticed*', said Brummell, who became the arbiter of men's fashion during the Regency period. Showing meticulous stylistic leadership, he popularised modern trousers, starched cravats and waistcoats, while shunning gentlemen's stockings. His showy wit, refinement and elegant dress sense brought him the nickname 'Beau'. His legacy endures

in shirt-makers and clothing stores in the surrounding St James's neighbourhood.

4. William Morris (1834-1896)

Textile designer, artist and social reformer, Morris was at the forefront of the English Arts & Crafts movement fashionable in the 1880s and supported the Pre-Raphaelite Brotherhood's approach to art. His dress fabrics and wallpaper designs are still appreciated today. A visit to his home transports you to a pre-industrial 'golden age' of craftsmanship and production based on traditional, manual techniques.

5. Design Museum

London-born designer and restauranteur, Conran (1931-) made his name with distinctively modern housewares and home décor. His Habitat chain of stores helped modernise British homes. In 1989, he pioneered a gastronomic cultural quarter in London's not-yet-trendy Docklands, in which he also located a Design Museum. From 2016, the museum's new location in Kensington's creative quarter will showcase even more examples of contemporary product, industrial, graphic, fashion and architectural design.

6. Eltham Palace

Founded in late eighteenth century by a Huguenot manufacturer of silk textiles, in the early twentieth century Courtauld's became the world's leading producer of man-made fibres, such as rayon. Stephen and his Hungarian-Italian wife Virginia restored the medieval palace at Eltham, adding a wing in the fashionable art deco style and the latest in luxury domestic gadgets. Today, their beautiful former home and gardens are open to the public.

And when we're back in town, let's spin across to the Courtauld Gallery in Somerset House, Strand to appreciate one of London's fine art collections, with works by Manet, Gauguin, Monet, Van Gogh, Cézanne, Degas and others.

7. a. – viii; b. – iii; c. – vii; d. – v; e. – i; f. – iv; g. – vi; h. – ii

8. True
In 1849, Lock & Co. first stocked a practical protective head covering for gamekeepers employed by the landowner Edward Coke. This design became the basis for bowler hats – the symbol of City gentlemen – later worn and thrown with malice by villain Auric Goldfinger's less-than-gentlemanly bodyguard in the 1964 Bond film.

Lock also made signature hats for Admiral Lord Nelson (Bicorne with built-in eye-shade), Oscar Wilde (Fedora), and Sir Winston Churchill (Homburg). Currently holding Royal Warrants for services to the Duke of Edinburgh and the Prince of Wales, Lock made fitments for the crown used during Queen Elizabeth II's coronation ceremony in 1953.

9. Museum of Brands, Packaging and Advertising
A visit to this museum of consumer marketing evokes fond memories of much-loved brands and advertising. The collection includes items dating back to the birth of modern marketing in the nineteenth century, along with more contemporary objects, reminding us of London's leading role in creative services and the foundations of modern consumer society.

10. Twiggy being shot on location by Terence Donovan (overlooked by a surprised passer-by)

The three-part composition was installed in 2012. Acclaimed photographer and film-maker Donovan's Mayfair studio evokes the 'Swinging Sixties', a time when London's Carnaby Street and Chelsea were trendsetting centres for stylish clothing and London-born model Twiggy was one of the era's defining faces. Later, Donovan worked here on photos of Diana, Princess of Wales, as well as with other top fashion names.

Donovan's studio (1978–96) in this sleepy West End mews is close to the flagship fashion stores on Bond Street, as well as Mayfair boutiques of several of the hottest fashion designers.

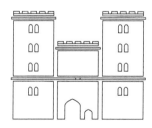

TOUR 17

Screen & Stage

London plays a leading role in many films and TV productions and offers arguably the world's finest selection of theatre, music, dance and opera. Whether your taste is for live performance or pre-recorded, let's go out and enjoy the show.

1. Which franchise of eight magical films was shot in studios at Leavesden?

2. Which long-running series of films features Vauxhall Cross – headquarters of Britain's secret service MI6 – located on the Thames upriver from Westminster?

3. Which theatre complex in Bankside realises the vision of American actor and film director Sam Wanamaker?

4. Europe's largest multi-arts and performance centre is in London. What is its name?

5. Which world-famous venue is shared by The Royal Opera and The Royal Ballet?

6. Which record-breaking musical production has been running in London since September 1986?

7. Which 'People's Palace' on a north London hill is known as the birthplace of TV broadcasts?

8. Which central London royal park has a permanent open-air theatre?

9. What is 'Savoy opera', a form of theatrical entertainment that began in London in the late nineteenth century?

10. Which iconic London location has appeared in these Bollywood films?

- *Kabhi Khushie Kabhie Gham* (2001)
- *Bhagam Bhag* (2006)
- *I See You* (2006)
- *Salaam-E-Ishq* (2007)

And that brings the curtain down on this tour.

Answers: Tour 17

1. Harry Potter

The films of J.K. Rowling's best-selling books about the adventures of a young wizard were produced at Warner Bros studios north of London, where many sets, props and special effects are on permanent display. Soho in central London is also home to VFX, sound, costume and post-production experts who pick up awards most years at the Oscars.

On your tour, your guide will conjure up a few of the many Harry Potter film locations in London.

2. James Bond - 007

Britain's secret intelligence service (MI6) is based next to Vauxhall Bridge, a setting used in several Bond films including a river chase in *Spectre*, total destruction in *Skyfall* and missile strike in *The World Is Not Enough*. That's only make-believe, so do take a good look during your tour of London film locations!

3. Shakespeare's Globe

Opened in 1997 after a campaign headed by Wanamaker (1919-1993), the Globe recreates the seventeenth-century O-shaped theatre of actor-playwright William Shakespeare. Standing near the site of its predecessor, the Globe's mission is to entertain and educate modern audiences about stagecraft and the stage classics. A second space named after Sam Wanamaker offers a unique experience - candlelit productions during the autumn-winter seasons when the open-roofed Globe presents that three-act tragedy known as 'British weather'.

4. The Barbican Centre

This cultural complex includes theatre stages, concert hall for contemporary and classical music, art gallery, multi-screen cinema, library with arts and music resources, and a conservatoire to train the next generation of talented performers. As the UK's third largest supporter of the arts, the City of London Corporation keeps hitting all the right notes. 'Brava!'

5. The Royal Opera House (or simply 'Covent Garden')

Standing on the site of an opera and ballet house built in 1732, the current façade, foyer and auditorium date from 1858, with extensive modernisation in the 1990s adding the beautiful cast iron and glass hall recycled from the former Covent Garden flower market. Several seats include a small screen for an electronic libretto system appreciated by true devotees.

Leading international opera singers and ballet companies perform in this magnificent setting.

6. *The Phantom of the Opera*

The phenomenon that is *Phantom* is based on a French novel set to music by Lord (Andrew) Lloyd Webber with lyrics by Charles Hart and additions from Richard Stilgoe. Its record-breaking run in London's West End has outlasted five British prime ministers. With productions in 150 cities in 30 countries, *Phantom* also holds the longevity record on New York's Broadway.

For an '*Encore!*' your guide notes the neat symmetry of this opera-themed production playing on the site of eighteenth-century Haymarket Opera House, where Handel's first opera in England was performed.

7. Alexandra Palace

In 1935, the British Broadcasting Corporation leased space in this large hill-top entertainment venue to make the world's first regular public television transmissions and TV news broadcasts continued until 1969. In the early 1960s, passage of the first satellite to pass over London was described from an outside broadcast on the roof. Hill-top masts are still used for terrestrial TV, radio and DAB transmissions.

Opened by Queen Victoria in 1873 as north London's answer to Crystal Palace across town, the unmatched Italianate architecture of 'Ally Pally' soon became a popular attraction. However, fire soon caused extensive damage.

An on-going project is restoring part of the TV studios and entertainment hall. There are opportunities to visit on selective dates and see a collection of historical television equipment.

8. Regent's Park

Britain's only permanent open-air professional stage offers four productions from May–September. Make time before the evening show to enjoy this lovely park's fragrant rose garden, go boating, or look for the resident hedgehogs.

After all that, you will be ready to see the stars come out in the 1,200-seat theatre.

9. Comic opera written by Gilbert & Sullivan

In 1881, impresario Richard D'Oyly Carte built the Savoy Theatre on the site of thirteenth-century Count of Savoy's London residence as a venue for popular musical productions from the fertile pens of composer Arthur Sullivan and librettist W.S. Gilbert. Gilbert & Sullivan's thirteen major works include *The Mikado*, *HMS Pinafore* and *The Pirates of Penzance*. Less fashionable today, they influenced modern musical theatre that thrives in London's Theatreland.

The adjacent Savoy Hotel was opened by D'Oyly Carte in 1889 to offer state-of-the-art accommodation and dining to visitors to his theatre. That meant (gasp!) electric lighting and lifts, and an ensuite bathroom in most of the guest rooms.

10. Tower Bridge

The Bollywood film industry produces more than 1,000 films a year from its base in Mumbai, India – a larger volume of films than Hollywood although not yet generating as much global revenue. With exotic overseas locations often playing a major part in storylines, London's iconic locations serve as backdrops for spectacular song and dance numbers.

Nollywood (based in Nigeria) now also produces more films than Hollywood, so maybe it's only a matter of time before London guides offer an even greater variety of location tours!

Find a Blue Badge guide to show you locations from Tower Bridge to Southall.

Undergound & Overground

With a surface area of 610 sq. miles London simply could not function without its many forms of transport. This round tests your knowledge of our city's transport systems.

1. Which city has the world's oldest underground passenger railway?

    a. Moscow   d. Tokyo
    b. Mexico City   e. Chicago
    c. Madrid   f. London

2. Which mid-nineteenth century station has been given a twenty-first-century makeover as the terminus for international high-speed services to Belgium and France?

3. What innovation did George Shillibeer bring to London's streets in 1829?

4. What percentage of London's Tube network runs underground?

    a. 35%   c. 55%
    b. 45%   d. 65%

5. What form of transport – much loved by two-term mayor Boris Johnson – received major boosts under his administration in 2010 and 2016?

6. What is the name of London's newest underground rail line opening in 2017/18?

7. Which famous father and son led the project that built the Thames Tunnel, the world's first tunnel under a navigable river when opened in 1843?

8. Which elegantly engineered steel footbridge connects St Paul's Cathedral with Bankside's Tate Modern Gallery and Shakespeare's Globe Theatre?

9. What transport system spans the Thames between North Greenwich and the Royal Docks?

10. In 2017, a section of underground railway forming part of London's industrial heritage will be opened to the public for the first time. What is it called?

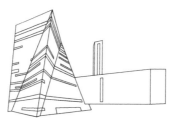

*Let's head back above ground and
get ready for our next tour.*

Answers: Tour 18

1. f. London
Developed from 1863, London's underground rail network used steam locomotives until the advent of electric trains. Relentless consolidation and expansion has created today's Tube network of 11 lines, 270 stations and 1.3 billion passenger journeys (2015).

2. St Pancras International
Opened in 1868 as London terminus of the Midland Railway, the station's spectacular cast-iron and glass train shed and brick vaults were transformed in 2007 into a modern, international gateway. Combining Victorian engineering with contemporary design excellence, there is no better place to start our high-speed exploration of London's railway heritage.

3. Public buses
Borrowing an idea seen in France, Shillibeer introduced regular services in horse-drawn buses at an affordable fare for everyone (Latin '*omnibus*'). London's public bus service now records 2 billion passenger journeys a year. For a look at transport heritage, visit the London Transport Museum in Covent Garden and depot in Acton.

4. b. 45%
In spite of prominent 'Underground' signage, less than half of the 250-mile network runs underground. The oldest lines are close to the surface - hand-dug trenches covered over

with a roof ('cut and cover') until development of safer mining techniques enabled deep-bored tunnels – the 'Tube', as we now call the entire network. Beyond the centre where land was easier to obtain, the Tube expanded more cost-effectively above ground or by adopting existing steam railway track.

5. Bicycling

In 2010, during Mayor Johnson's first term in office, Transport for London (TfL) introduced its public bicycle hire scheme, dubbed 'Boris Bikes'; 43 million journeys were made in the first five years and in July 2015 a record 73,000 hires were achieved in a single day. When Johnson stepped down in 2016, twelve bicycle superhighways had been introduced on major routes to encourage safer use of precious road space and greater use of this two-wheeled, self-propelled form of exercise.

Time will tell whether the bikes get renamed as 'Sadiq Cycles'!

6. Crossrail (to be named the Elizabeth Line when it opens)

This west-east line includes 26 miles of new tunnels bored under central London – equivalent to an entire marathon course. During the busiest period of London's £14 billion construction initiative, Crossrail was Europe's largest infra-structure project. Access shafts and station upgrade works are visible throughout London as the countdown to opening continues.

Crossrail promises to speed up travel for commuters and visitors across much of the south-east and expand rail capacity significantly along a route from Reading in the west to Abbey Wood and Shenfield in the east – for example, 40 minutes from Heathrow Airport to Canary Wharf.

Regeneration of areas above Crossrail's route may already be seen on local walking tours. Visits below ground are being offered occasionally in the run-up to launching the service. After being granted development funding by the government in early 2016, planning and public consultation is accelerating for a second line running north-south to help the wider London and south-east region manage continuing population growth.

7. Marc Brunel and Isambard Kingdom Brunel

Conceived by Brunel Sr as a carriage and foot tunnel under the busy Thames docks, the Thames Tunnel is 1,300ft long, running at a depth of 75ft below the river surface measured at high tide. Opened after overcoming unparalleled financial and tunnelling challenges, it was a success as a foot tunnel and tourist attraction. However, lack of funds to build access for horse-drawn carts and vehicles led to its demise as railways captured a growing share of commercial freight. In 1865, the tunnel was acquired by a railway company and today connects TfL's Overground rail line between Rotherhithe and Wapping. After this short rail trip and seeing the Brunel Museum in Rotherhithe's incomplete access shaft, visitors find the story of this remarkable connection is anything but boring.

Incidentally, one of eight giant Crossrail tunnelling machines was named *Sophia* after the wife of Marc and mother of Isambard.

8. Millennium Bridge

Opened in 2000 to celebrate the new millennium, the bridge was intended to improve access to new attractions on Bankside. A stunning design was executed by Foster & Partners, Sir Anthony Caro and Arup, and an estimated 80-100,000 people eagerly crossed on the first day. Unfortunately, this caused an unsettling swaying sensation and the bridge was immediately closed for re-engineering. Thanks to a clever system of dampers, visitors today enjoy some of London's best views from the bridge and will be swayed only by the many entertaining sights and sounds now in easy reach on the river's north and south banks.

9. Cable-car

Opened in 2012, the cable-car connected venues during the Olympic and Paralympic Games. Subsequently renamed as the Emirates Air Line, this unusual urban commuter link also attracts visitors seeking an unconventional perspective over London's continuing Docklands regeneration.

10. Post Office railway or 'mail rail'

A 6.5-mile railway running from Whitechapel to Paddington was opened in 1927 as a private facility transferring mail bags between sorting centres. Driverless trains ran on narrow-gauge tracks until declining volumes of mail made the system uneconomic. As part of the new Postal Museum near Mount Pleasant sorting office in Clerkenwell, a section of railway mothballed in 2003 is to reopen. No doubt it will deliver a 'First Class' visitor experience!

TOUR 19

Royalty & Government

This tour looks at queens and kings, rulers, residences and respected royal retailers. Are you ready?

1. After financing its reconstruction, in 1066 which king became the first person to be buried in Westminster Abbey?

2. Where are the royal and state regalia known as the 'Crown Jewels' kept on display?

3. Whose official residence is Mansion House?

    a. Prime Minister   d. Anne, Princess Royal
    b. Duke of Wellington   e. Lord Mayor of London
    c. Charles, Prince of Wales f. Bishop of London

4. Which palace is the London home to the Duke and Duchess of Cambridge and their young family?

5. Before London definitively became England's capital in the twelfth century, which city was considered most prominent?

    a. Winchester   d. Norwich
    b. Manchester   e. Oxford
    c. Exeter   f. York

6. What royal connection is shared by these companies: Berry Bros & Rudd (wine, spirits), Lobb (shoes, leather goods), Selfridge's (food, household goods) and Fortnum & Mason (food, provisions)?

7. True or false? The Silent Ceremony is so called because the audience must listen in silence.

8. The Banqueting House is the last remaining part of which central London palace destroyed by fire in 1698?

9. Who is the only king or queen to have been born and to die at Buckingham Palace?

10. Which south-east London palace was used extensively to raise royal children from the fourteenth to the sixteenth centuries?

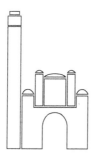

It's time to head back into central London for our next tour.

Answers: Tour 19

1. King Edward the Confessor (*c.* 1003–1066)

No sooner were the masons out than the (ex-)monarch was in. Pious Edward was laid to rest in the recently opened abbey on Thorn Ey (Island) next to his palace on the river at Westminster. The coronation church was rebuilt in the thirteenth–fourteenth centuries in the Gothic style. Edward's shrine is surrounded by sixteen rulers of England (plus one queen of Scotland), by hundreds of other people from 'the Illustrious' to ordinary members of Westminster's local community, and by the grave of our Unknown Warrior.

2. Tower of London

The Crown Jewels are a working collection of precious regalia that are used on state occasions. Many items are on permanent display in a strong-room inside the Tower, where this glittering collection has been delighting visitors for three centuries. Look out for the 530.4 carat 'First Star of Africa', the world's largest, flawless, pure cut diamond, and a twelfth-century spoon used to anoint monarchs during their coronation service.

   Simply an unmissable collection of priceless treasures!

3. e. Lord Mayor

The grand eighteenth-century edifice facing the Bank of England and the Royal Exchange in the City's heart is home for every Lord Mayor during their one-year term in office. Banquets and the receiving of important guests take place here. The Egyptian Hall is a masterpiece of Palladian neo-classical style and a world-class collection of gold- and silver-plate and other precious objects reflects the Mayoralty and City's historic stature. If you are still in two minds about a guided visit, there's also a notable collection of seventeenth-century Dutch Old Master paintings.

4. Kensington Palace

With Prince William working as a pilot in the air ambulance service in Norfolk, Amner Hall on the Queen's Sandringham estate is the family's usual residence. In London, Kensington Palace is home for the Duke of Cambridge, his wife Kate and their children George and Charlotte.

King William III and Queen Mary II established Kensington as a royal palace and later, this was where young Victoria lived until becoming queen in 1837. The story of royal residents is told in a wing of the palace open year-round.

5. a. Winchester

From the ninth century until after the Norman invasion of 1066, Winchester was regarded as England's capital and King William I had himself crowned in both cities. London's growing commercial importance and location, combined with the new regime's system of government, helped establish London as the principal city of England.

6. They hold at least one Royal Warrant of Appointment

Royal Warrants are granted by the Lord Chamberlain (head of the royal household) to a very select group of companies that meet stringent criteria including several years of service to households of the Queen, Duke of Edinburgh or Prince of Wales. There are currently approximately 900 businesses, with two-thirds of warrants awarded by the Queen. Arms of the awarding senior member of the Royal Family may be displayed on premises as an outward sign of their good standing and a tour of (say) St James's and Piccadilly soon brings you into sight of several of these businesses.

7. False

This civic ceremony in November in Guildhall formally admits an incoming Lord Mayor of the City of London to their year in office. Imbued with over 800 years of mayoral history, it is open to the public, although obtaining a ticket requires application in September. It is never televised.

Is it really conducted in silence? There are no long speeches, recitations or shouts of 'Hurrah!' – just a short declaration uttered aloud that confirms willingness to accept the office and care for the Mansion House. There is plenty of hat doffing, bowing, presenting of insignia, pen scratching as signatures are signed, and jangling of ceremonial regalia as honorary officers process in a stately fashion wearing traditional robes of office.

8. Whitehall

The palace has (mostly) gone but its name lives on as a synonym for the national government quarter. Architect Inigo Jones's early seventeenth-century Banqueting House is notable for being the first Palladian neo-classical building completed in England. Its fine ceiling was painted by Flemish artist Peter-Paul Rubens and it was through a window in this grand room that King Charles I stepped onto a stage to be beheaded publicly in 1649.

9. King Edward VII (born 1841, reigned 1901-10)

The eldest child of Queen Victoria and Prince Albert, Edward was born soon after his parents had moved in, establishing this as the principal royal residence in town. In 1902, the elderly new king bravely underwent emergency surgery for peritonitis in the palace, but died there in 1910.

10. Eltham Palace

Eltham is something of a hidden gem. Its fifteenth-century hall dates from King Edward IV's reign, who considered this his favourite palace. Buildings, garden and hunting grounds had been extended in the fourteenth century by Edward II and his wife Isabella ('The She-Wolf of France') for their son (Edward III). Henry VIII spent much of his boyhood here in the late fifteenth century.

Eltham Palace is now managed by English Heritage and is easily accessible from central London by public transport.

TOUR 20

High & Low

Guides always recommend 'Look up!' and with all those cranes visible on London's skyline, there is plenty of high-rise construction. This tour looks above our heads and below our feet.

1. What is Westminster's Elizabeth Tower usually called?

2. What great events in London's history are commemorated by The Monument?

3. Match these modern buildings with their architect or engineer:

   a. 'Gherkin' (30 St Mary Axe)
   b. 'Walkie-Talkie' (20 Fenchurch Street)
   c. Aquatics Centre (Queen Elizabeth Olympic Park)
   d. 'The Cheesegrater' (Leadenhall Street)
   e. Number 1 Poultry (Queen Victoria Street and Poultry)
   f. One New Change (Cheapside and New Change)

   i. Sir James Stirling
   ii. Jean Nouvel
   iii. Lord Foster and Ken Shuttleworth
   iv. Dame Zaha Hadid
   v. Rafael Viñoly
   vi. Lord Rogers

4. Name the tallest building in western Europe.

5. True or false? The London Eye is the world's tallest Ferris wheel.

6. Which of these buildings and structures was not designed by a member of the Gilbert Scott dynasty of architects?

   a. Battersea Power Station
   b. Albert Memorial
   c. Natural History Museum
   d. Guildhall Yard complex
   e. Red public telephone kiosks
   f. Waterloo Bridge
   g. Midland Grand Hotel (now St Pancras Renaissance Hotel)
   h. Foreign & Commonwealth Office

7. Name the City's high-rise residential district rebuilt according to the principles of architect Le Corbusier.

8. Why are there no electricity pylons visible on the Queen Elizabeth Olympic Park?

9. Which civil engineer devised a ground-breaking network of sewage pipes and treatment plants that improved public health in the 1860s?

10. Which 150-year-old architectural gem in Westminster needs 'the mother of all repair budgets'?

*Let's rest those strained neck muscles before
we take a look at London's pet animals.*

Answers: Tour 20

1. 'Big Ben'

Added to the new Houses of Parliament building in 1859, 'Big Ben' is the large bell that chimes the hours. Cast in east London, it was named after either Sir Benjamin Hall, the lanky engineer in charge of construction, or a heavy-weight boxer. Queen Elizabeth's Diamond (60th) Jubilee in 2012 was marked by renaming this much-photographed tower but 'Big Ben' will endure, no doubt.

A three-year programme of repairs starting in 2017 will silence the bell's distinctive 'bong' that marks the hours, although it may still be struck on special occasions.

2. The Great Fire of 1666 that destroyed 80% of the City, and its subsequent reconstruction

Designed by Sir Christopher Wren and Dr Robert Hooke, the world's tallest free-standing stone column is topped by a flaming gilt urn. At 202ft, its height marks the exact distance to the fire's starting place in Thomas Farynor's bakery. The column was erected in 1671-77 alongside the principal road then leading to London Bridge.

Climb the 311-step staircase to the viewing platform and earn a certificate to prove it!

3. a. – iii; b. – v; c. – iv; d. – vi; e. – i; f. – ii

4. The Shard, London Bridge Street, SE1

Towering 1,016ft above Borough, this 'vertical crystal palace' of 11,000 glass panels was designed by Italian architect

Renzo Piano in the form of a spire-like splinter. Its seventy-two habitable floors accommodate a hotel, health club, restaurants, offices and apartments. A three-storey viewing space has unbeatable views over Greater London – on clear days, as far as Windsor Castle and Heathrow Airport – while the outlook from the restaurants' toilets is truly special! The Shard and adjacent low-rise 'Baby Shard' are the centrepiece of the wider redevelopment of London Bridge Quarter.

Before opening in 2013, it had attracted its first resident, an urban fox that resisted removal and has become The Shard's mascot with the name 'Romeo'.

5. False

In fact, false on two counts. Erected to celebrate the millennium in 2000, the revolving platform was designed by husband and wife architectural team Julia Marks and David Barfield. Ferris wheels are supported on both sides, but this riverside wheel is suspended from a single, shoreside column. And at 443ft it is not the tallest either – that honour currently goes to 'High Roller' in Las Vegas, USA (550ft).

6. c. Natural History Museum was designed by Alfred Waterhouse.

b., g. and h. are the work of George Gilbert Scott.

a., e. and f. are by Giles Gilbert Scott.

d. is by Richard Gilbert Scott.

7. The Barbican

A barbican is a watchtower on a walled city. This 40-acre estate north of London's former wall comprises low-rise blocks and urban precincts surmounted by three

Brutalist-style, concrete apartment blocks – Europe's tallest residential towers when constructed.

Swiss-French architect and urban planner Le Corbusier's (1887-1965) ideas were reflected in the scheme by Chamberlin, Powell & Bon to redevelop this post-war bomb-site as a city centre residential and cultural estate. Now 4,000 people live there, comprising about half of all residents of the City of London.

8. Pylons are in underground utilities tunnels

Decontamination and beautification work to prepare the site for the London 2012 Games (and future use as a park) included digging two 3.7-mile tunnels to conceal fifty-two less-than-lovely electricity pylons. Spoil sufficient to fill Wembley Stadium was dug out and you may be shocked to learn that all that electrical cable would stretch from London to Nottingham, a distance of 127 miles!

9. Sir Joseph Bazalgette (1819-91)

After a particularly unpleasant and infectious period during the hot summer of 1858, civic authorities wanted action. Bazalgette was commissioned to come up with a comprehensive response to the threat to public health from river-borne diseases such as cholera – a disease that caused 10,000 London deaths in the 1850s. Bazalgette's solution reclaimed land along the Thames foreshore for massive low-level sewer pipes and exploited natural gradients to move household waste out east for removal by the tide. Gardens and roads were added above ground along Westminster's Victoria Embankment, Lambeth's Albert Embankment and Chelsea Embankment.

Alongside these sewer pipes were installed sections of underground railway, but that is not why one of our Tube lines is called 'Bakerloo'!

10. Palace of Westminster, home to the Houses of Parliament (and 'Big Ben')

Designed in Gothic Revival style by Charles Barry and Augustus Pugin, this well-known nineteenth-century edifice is home to 'the mother of all parliaments'. Officials and elected representatives must decide how to effect major repairs needed to conserve the fabric of this UNESCO World Heritage Site, while making it fit for purpose in the twenty-first century.

Depending on the building's use, tours are conducted at specific times throughout the year by a team of specially trained Blue Badge guides and resident staff, who interpret this historic site from 1097 up to modern times. You will be walking in the footsteps of national politicians and world statesmen.

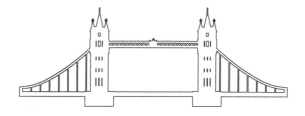

TOUR 21

Pooches & Pets

Londoners' infatuation with animals of all kinds is not just a modern phenomenon. Let's now poop off to scoop up a few of the beastly beauties to be found all across London.

1. What breed of dog is associated with Queen Elizabeth II?

2. Domhnall is the current mascot of one of the leading regiments of the British Army. Which one?

3. Which unusual creature is the favourite pet of former Mayor of London, Ken Livingstone?

   a. Capybara   d. Slow-worm
   b. Sloth   e. Newt
   c. Terrapin

4. Which famous London store supplied an alligator for Sir Noël Coward and an elephant for Ronald Reagan?

5. What type of once-popular London pet was raced at Walthamstow Stadium?

6. Which artist kept a menagerie in his Chelsea home that included a pet wombat called 'Top'?

7. What type of animal was Mah-Jongg, a pet who lived at Eltham Palace in the 1930s?

8. To whom was Giro *Ein treuer Begleiter* ('A faithful companion')?

9. In which of the central London parks will you find Pet Cemetery?

10 What exotic beast famously escaped from Charles Jamrach's East End animal emporium in 1857?

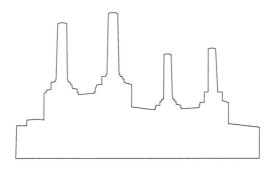

Well, that tour got a bit wild, didn't it? Let's take a moment to rest before heading out together one final time.

Answers: Tour 21

1. Corgi

Her Majesty's parents, King George VI and Queen Elizabeth the Queen Mother, started the royal tradition of keeping corgis. At the time of writing the royal household is home to Holly and Willow. Corgis also have been cross-bred with dachshunds to create 'dorgis'.

These canines follow in the paws of princely pooches that include pugs, Labradors, collies and, self-evidently, King Charles spaniels. A terrier belonging to the late King Edward VII even walked behind his royal master's funeral cortège.

2. Irish Guards

Since the early twentieth century when Brian Boru was presented to the regiment, their mascot has been an Irish Wolfhound. Domhnall (Gaelic for 'World Leader') has been on duty since 2013 and is often seen on parade with the soldiers. His star turns come in March at the St Patrick's Day parade and in June, when Domhnall accompanies the regiment wearing their ceremonial finery from Wellington Barracks to Horse Guards for the spectacle of Trooping the Colour that celebrates the Sovereign's Official Birthday.

3. e. Newt

Livingstone confesses readily to a lifelong fascination with these little native amphibians. Indeed, he kept reptiles and amphibians of various kinds during his childhood growing up in south London, a 'my newt' habit (as one might say) that sustains him into his advanced adulthood.

4. Harrods

With its motto *Omnia Omnibus Ubique* – 'All Things for All People, Everywhere' – the Knightsbridge store was famous for supplying the world with domestic and exotic creatures.

For instance, in 1951 a Canadian actress bought an alligator as a Christmas gift for Coward, the flamboyant English playwright, composer, director, actor and singer. In 1967, a baby elephant was ordered by Reagan, at that time governor of California and future US President, who needed one for a Republican party rally (as you do). Legend relates that when Reagan rang Harrods to ask if they sold the animal that is the symbol of his political party, he received the reply: 'Would that be African or Indian, sir?' Now THAT'S service!

5. Greyhounds

Between 1933-2008, greyhound racing was synonymous with 'the Stow'. After the sport arrived from the USA in the 1920s, London had tracks in Haringey, Wimbledon, Romford and Crayford where trained dogs chased a mechanical 'rabbit' around a track and many Londoners kept and train greyhounds and whippets – 'the poor man's race horse'.

I'd love to tell you that you'll find Walthamstow on the Isle of Dogs but that definitely would be a 'fishy' fact!

6. Dante Gabriel Rossetti

Rossetti was a leading light in the Pre-Raphaelite Brotherhood. After the tragic death of his wife, he took to keeping a noisy and increasingly noisome mix of exotic animals in his Chelsea residence-cum-zoo.

Australian marsupials were very much a rarity in Victorian England, so wombats made the perfect hipster accessory.

But why stop at just one wombat when you can also possess racoon, armadillo, woodchuck, wallaby, kangaroo and zebu? His plans to acquire an African elephant were truncated before his irritated neighbours could say 'Tsk, tsk!'

Rossetti sketched Top held by Jane Morris, the beautiful model wife of William Morris, philosopher of the PRB's distinctive aesthetic style: DGR's two muses combined in a single sketch.

7. Ring-tailed lemur

Stephen and Virginia Courtauld bought the lemur at – yes, you guessed – Harrods as a companion in their childless marriage. 'Jongy' was given the run of their sumptuous art deco residence, including a special bamboo ladder to access his centrally heated sleeping quarters directly from the public rooms. The lemur's likeness also appears in a mural painting commissioned for the house and carved into wooden bosses in the conserved medieval hall.

8. German Ambassador Leopold von Hoesch

Von Hoesch was the charming, Anglophile ambassador of the Weimar Republic of Germany. In 1932, he brought over his beloved pet terrier, who shared the embassy near Buckingham Palace until Giro chewed through a cable in the back garden and was electrocuted; his resting place is marked by a small gravestone close to the site.

9. Hyde Park

Behind Victoria Gate off Bayswater Road, your guide will point out a hidden garden of rest for much-missed pets.

Private tours show visitors evocative headstones in memory of 300 tenderly named animal companions. Here we find Pupsey, Moussoo and Chin Chin on their eternal walkies with Bobbit, Scamp and Priny.

One may only speculate on unintended storylines to be conjured out of near neighbours Trix and Smut, or Pomme de Terre, Chips, Fatty and Ruby Heart.

10. Bengal tiger

Jamrach's father built a successful exotic animal trade in Germany, and Charles came to England to develop their menagerie in the world's busiest port. Through international suppliers and contacts in London's docks, Jamrach ensured a prolific trade importing exotic creatures. Dante Gabriel Rossetti was one of his customers and Jamrach found buyers among the nation's zoos and private owners in those unscrupulous times, when animal welfare and conservation were rarely considered.

In 1857, a newly-arrived tiger succeeded in breaking free from its cage in Jamrach's yard. Picking up a passing child in its jaws, the tiger prowled menacingly down St George's Street towards the dockside, causing public panic. The fearsome animal eventually was recaptured and the very fortunate child escaped relatively unscathed. A statue depicting the tiger and its intended snack today stands near Tobacco Dock in commemoration of the day that the East End nearly became 'Feast. End'.

It would be lovely to be able to tell you that the tiger statue lurks near a zebra crossing* but that would be 'a complete porky' (Cockney: 'pork pie' meaning 'a lie')!

*A zebra crossing is a black and white-striped area across a public highway, where vehicles must stop to allow pedestrians to cross safely. Exactly the kind of safe crossing point you may expect your Blue Badge guide to look for on your tour.

TOUR 22

Lost & Found

This final tour looks at things that have been uncovered or have disappeared over the years.

1. Which large Roman structure was found in 1988 during the construction of Guildhall Art Gallery?

2. Are there still farm animals to be found anywhere in central London?

3. True or false? Walking on the Thames foreshore at low tide is permitted.

4. The waters of which 'lost river' flow through the Clerk's Well in Islington?

5. The remains of which unfortunate former residents have been rediscovered in Southwark's Cross Bones burial ground?

6. Approximately how many ancient objects were found in 2014 by archaeologists working on a small section of the site of a new office block at Walbrook?

7. Although most of architect Sir John Soane's buildings have been lost, where is the museum dedicated to his work?

8. Which north London house recently revealed interiors in the original colour scheme designed by the Adam Brothers?

9. What did John Harrison invent in the eighteenth century that stopped travellers getting lost?

10. What was unexpectedly discovered – and subsequently replaced – during archaeological investigations on the building site at 30 Street Mary Axe ('The Gherkin')?

And so our programme of themed tours around London ends, appropriately, back with the Romans – founders of this great metropolis nearly 2,000 years ago.

It's been a pleasure showing you around my home town. There's still plenty left to discover, so do come back soon and explore more of the area with a Blue Badge guide!

Answers: Tour 22

1. Amphitheatre

Londinium's 'lost' amphitheatre accommodated 6,000 citizens attending gladiatorial combat, sports, civic ceremonies, animal fights and public executions until the decline of Romano-British culture from the fifth century. Exposed during construction of the City of London's art gallery in Guildhall Yard, well-preserved remains are accessed through the gallery's lower level.

2. Yes

While central London's fields and farms have been built over, long ago, 'city farms' with animals to feed, pet, ride or simply enjoy are to be found in urban districts from Vauxhall, Hackney, Mudchute, Kentish Town, Hounslow to Surrey Docks.

Also visit London Zoo in Regent's Park and discover how the Zoological Society of London is leading conservation initiatives across our planet to prevent more species from being lost forever.

3. True – with due precaution

The Thames's tide rises and falls by 22ft twice daily, exposing sections of foreshore where 'mudlarking' to find old objects or simply strolling by the water can be fun. Consult your guide about sensible precautions and permits for restricted activities, such as metal-detecting on private land. Do watch out for those fast-flowing tides.

4. The Fleet

On its route from Hampstead towards the Thames, the Fleet gave rise to several wells around Farringdon. Best known is the Clerk's Well, named after clerks (clerics or parish priests) once numerous here on the city fringes – the district of Clerkenwell. Since 1924, the well rediscovered in Farringdon Lane in the foundations of a building has been kept in public view.

5. Paupers and prostitutes

Preparations for an extension of a Tube line in the 1990s uncovered a forgotten burial ground containing approximately 15,000 bodies of unfortunate locals, who died in poverty or from sexually transmitted diseases. Today's residents are campaigning for the site's preservation, holding regular vigils at the burial ground's gates and creating the 'Goose Garden' in remembrance of 'Winchester Geese,' who once worked in the local sex trade.

6. 10,000 Roman objects

Before construction of foundations for Bloomberg Place in the heart of the City, specialists from Museum of London Archaeology raced against time to unearth a hoard of objects dating back to the Roman era. These included jewellery and organic material (leather; wooden door) preserved by the anaerobic environment created by the 'lost' River Walbrook flowing through the site.

Hailed as 'the Pompeii of the north', the completed precinct will provide exhibition space for conserved treasures and reinstate a Mithraic temple located here since Roman times.

7. Lincoln's Inn Fields, WC2

Soane (1753-1837) was a highly regarded architect. He remodelled his townhouse to display his antiquities collection and to experiment with architectural theories, and it is open to visit as he left it. What remains locally of his work includes parts of the Bank of England, Dulwich Picture Gallery and Pitzhanger Manor in Ealing.

By the way, the classical marble canopy Soane designed above his family tomb in Old St Pancras churchyard later inspired Soane Museum Trustee Giles Gilbert Scott's design of our famous red telephone kiosks.

8. Kenwood House, Hampstead Lane, NW3

Acquired by leading judge Lord Mansfield, Kenwood House was redesigned in the late eighteenth century by the Adam Brothers in their signature neo-classical style. Later owners redecorated the interiors, until a recent conservation project revealed and restored the striking colours of the Adams' original décor.

This stately home is an elegant setting for several collections, including the Iveagh Bequest, a world-class exhibition of Dutch, French and English Old Masters assembled by Edward Cecil Guinness, 1st Earl of Iveagh. Considered the 'crown jewel' is a 'definitive' late self-portrait by Rembrandt (c. 1665), alongside major works by Vermeer, Van Dyck, Hals, Reynolds, Gainsborough, Turner and Larkin. Outside are lovely walks on the edge of Hampstead Heath and in parkland landscaped by the eighteenth-century English gardener Humphry Repton.

9. The marine chronometer, a portable sea clock and first effective means of measuring longitude

John Harrison (1693-1776) solved the problem of measuring exactly where you are in the world. Latitude (north-south) could be fixed but no reliable means existed to determine longitude (east-west) until the accuracy of Harrison's chronometer was proven in various weather conditions, at sea and on land.

Find the story of his chronometers and GMT in displays out east at Greenwich's Royal Observatory and Science Museum in South Kensington. He has a memorial – with an intriguing component, a bi-metallic strip – in the nave of Westminster Abbey, and is buried in Hampstead in north London, so you'll be travelling to all four prime compass points to find Harrison!

10. Grave of a Roman girl

Buried between AD 350-400 on the outer edge of Londinium – the thriving capital of this Roman province of Britannia – the body of a young Roman girl was unearthed during the construction of one of modern London's defining landmarks. Her remains were reinterred with due ceremony and a carved stone marks the spot.

RIP

(Latin: *Requiescat in pace*)

Also from the History Press

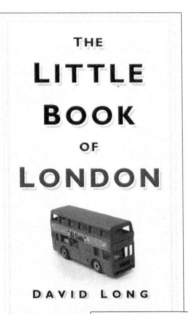

The destination for history
www.thehistorypress.co.uk